Women's Headdress and Hairstyles

in England from AD 600 to the present day

391.5

PEEBLES
COLLEGE LIBRARY

061-10

97105369

27. N

Women's Headdress and Hairstyles

in England from AD 600 to the present day

Georgine de Courtais

B T Batsford Ltd London

ID No. 97105369

Dewey No

Date Acq

First published 1973
© Georgine de Courtais 1973, 1986
Reprinted 1974
This revised edition published 1986

Filmset by Keyspools Ltd, Golborne, Lancs
Printed in Great Britain by
Anchor Brendon Ltd, Tiptree, Essex
for the publishers B. T. Batsford Ltd
4 Fitzhardinge Street, London W1H 0AH

ISBN 0 7134 5282 X

391·5
PETERLEE
COLLEGE LIBRARY
061-10

Contents

Acknowledgments

The author wishes to thank all who have given assistance and advice in connection with the preparation of this book and in particular the staff of Reading Public Library, the London Museum and the Imperial War Museum; the Rev. D. Aylmer Evans for permission to study his collection of rubbings of memorial brasses; Dr. Peter Cameloes for advice on sources of information about Anglo-Saxon costume; the late Mr. Digby Stone for checking many historical details and dates; and Mrs. Helen Spaven and Mrs. Shirley Billings for typing the manuscript.

Preface

The aim of this book is to provide a guide to the development of the headdresses, hairstyles and hats worn by Englishwomen since Saxon times together with some mention of the materials and methods used in their making. It is hoped that it will be of help to students of costume in schools and colleges and to all those who are interested for any reason in this important aspect of the feminine image. The brief introductions are intended to give only a general idea of the style of dress worn during each period and of its relationship to the headwear of the time. It is presumed that readers will already have some knowledge of the history of English costume.

In the free-for-all conditions in the world of fashion during recent years the wearing of a hat has become the exception and a fashionable hairstyle can hardly be said to exist if by the term "fashion" we mean a style that is adopted by the majority and which is sufficiently distinctive, in spite of individual differences, to be recognisable as belonging to a particular period. New styles and cuts may be introduced from time to time and hair pieces and wigs may be skilfully contrived, but women now wear their hair in any way they choose, long or short, straight or curly, in ponytail or bun, carefully set or in casual disarray. They can arrange a style to suit themselves, their way of life, and the amount of money and time they are prepared to spend. The latest "look" may change from season to season but at present the majority of women apparently prefer to cultivate their own.

G. de C.

Anglo-Saxon and Anglo-Norman
Seventh century A.D. to 1154 A.D.

Throughout Saxon times until well into the Norman period the costume of men and women underwent little change. The main function of clothing during those unsettled centuries was a practical one: fashion as we understand it did not exist. Social status was rigidly defined and any social emulation would have been unthinkable. In any case the mass of the population were in the main too poor and had insufficient leisure to be able to indulge in any taste for change or novelty in clothes. The wealthy ruling classes could show their superiority by wearing a more elaborate and richly decorated version of the general style of costume. The basic shape of garments remained the same for many centuries.

The costume of every Saxon woman consisted of three main garments: a chemise or under-garment, over which was worn a ground-length loose gown or *kirtle* which had long close-fitting sleeves; over this again was worn the *super tunic*, also loose and ground-length but often pulled up to knee-length by means of a sash or girdle. The sleeves of this garment were fairly wide and short enough to expose those of the gown. The cloak or mantle was square or rectangular in shape and was fastened at the throat. Very long trailing cloaks were worn by the nobility, as also were the "closed" mantles which had a hole in the centre or near to one edge so that they could be slipped over the head without a fastening.

Wool was the material used for all garments and linen was available for the wealthy. English-women were famed for their needlework and bands of embroidery in coloured and gold and silver thread appeared on hems, sleeve and neck edges and occasionally as panels down the fronts of super tunics.

No Saxon woman ever revealed her hair. Whatever her rank her head and neck were at all times heavily swathed in the folds of the *haefods-ragel* or head-rail.

The advent of the Normans brought few changes in the style of costume of the majority of the people of England. The main difference as far as women were concerned was that the head-rail, or *couvre-chef* as it was now called, was smaller. The first example of what might be termed "fashion" appeared in the reign of William II when garments and sleeves of extreme length were adopted by some of the well-to-do.

In the reign of Henry I the signs of increasing prosperity and more settled conditions were reflected in the dress of the nobility with a greater use of fur and imported materials such as silk.

Although women continued to wear the three garments and the cloak or mantle already described, a certain figure consciousness now became apparent, and by 1130 clothes were being shaped to fit more closely to the body. The gown, although remaining fairly full in the skirt, was shaped down to the hips by various means, the neck being slit or cut low to reveal the chemise. The super tunic was also tighter in the bodice but this garment was now sometimes omitted. The taste for length still lingered in the form of long hanging cuffs to sleeves which were otherwise tight fitting, and the elaborate girdles which rested on the hips or encircled the waist with ends hanging nearly to the ground. Perhaps the most remarkable feature, however, was the arrangement of the hair in plaits of exaggerated length. Although this hairstyle was apparently adopted only by the young and by ladies of royal or noble status it may be regarded as a significant step in the evolution of fashion. For the first time for many centuries women had begun to discard the heavy draperies which concealed hair and figure.

Anglo-Saxon

Throughout the Anglo-Saxon period only young unmarried girls wore their long hair loose and flowing and without any covering. All other women without exception kept their hair entirely hidden beneath the veil or head-rail, although it is probable that in the privacy of their homes they did not always cover their heads. Under the veil the hair was either worn loose or was braided and secured with hair bindings and pins with ornamented heads. These pins were also used to keep the veils in position. The veil was worn in a number of different ways. One of the earliest versions consisted of a circle or occasionally a square of fabric with a circular hole cut out to frame the face, whilst the rest of the material was folded or draped over the head and shoulders according to the taste of the wearer **(Figs. 1 and 3)**.

A more usual method of wearing the veil consisted of a rectangular length of material with an end fastened to one shoulder and then draped across the throat and over the head. Sometimes one side of the rectangle was cut in such a way as to form a semi-circular shape which was placed over the head and arranged in folds **(Fig. 2)**. These smaller veils were made of light-weight fabric such as silk or cambric, a fine gauze-like linen. A less usual method of wearing the veil but one which would have had obvious advantages in cold and windy weather was to have a very long rectangle of material with the draped portion carried over the free hanging end and wrapped once or twice around the neck **(Fig. 4)**. Veils were pulled tight under the chin and fastened or knotted at the side of the head whilst working at spinning, weaving and house-hold tasks or on the land.

Head-tires or circlet of gold, either plain or set with jewels, could be worn by any Saxon woman of rank, for it was not until a much later date that coronets were a particular mark of distinction. Veils were worn either under or over crowns and circlets **(Fig. 3)**. Fillets or bands of material, either plain or embroidered in gold or coloured thread, were also worn round the head to keep the veils in position.

Fig. 5 shows Saxon pins and a bone comb with teeth along both sides. Combs resembling modern ones with one row of teeth were also used.

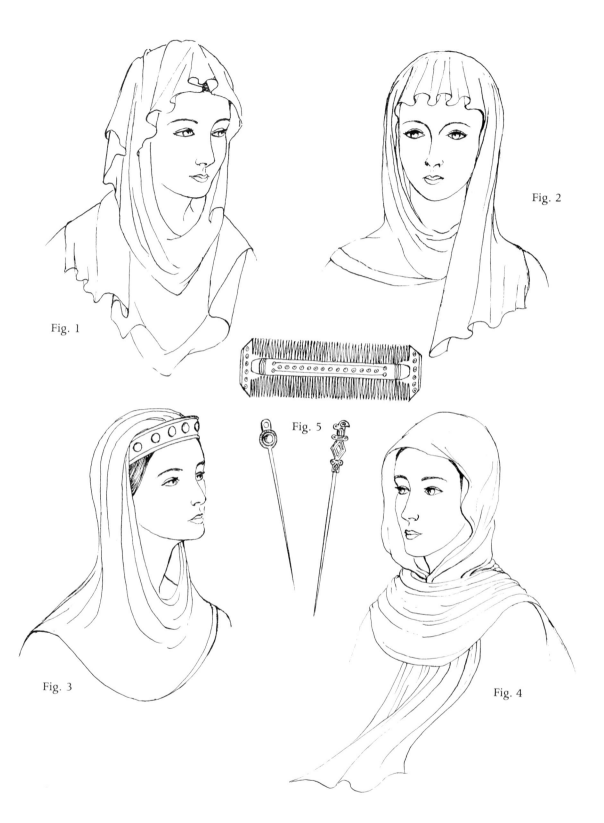

Fig. 1

Fig. 2

Fig. 5

Fig. 3

Fig. 4

Norman

During the first 50 years or so after the Norman invasion women continued to hide their hair under the veil or *couvre-chef*, as the head-rail was now called. There was little variation in the cut and methods of arrangement, although there was an increasing tendency for the *couvre-chef* to be worn hanging loose on either side of the face, exposing the throat and the neck of the gown. It was often kept in place by a simple fillet of cloth or metal, or in the case of noblewomen by a coronet.

Towards the end of the eleventh century narrow veils of extreme length appeared. The middle of the rectangle was placed on the head and kept in place by a fillet and the ends were often tied in knots to keep them clear of the ground. These veils were presumably made of silk or other lightweight material **(Fig. 8)**.

Sometime during the second quarter of the twelfth century and for the first time for many centuries women began to appear in public with their hair uncovered. It was parted in the centre and either arranged in two plaits which hung down in front or was divided into strands which were bound and interlaced with ribbons **(Fig. 6)**. Sometimes the side hair only was plaited whilst the rest hung freely down the wearer's back **(Fig. 7)**. Usually a small circular *couvre-chef* was worn and kept in position with a fillet or coronet **(Fig. 9)**. Extreme length was admired and the plaits which hung to the knees or in some cases to the ground were thickened and lengthened with false hair. The illusion of length was also obtained by encasing the tresses in silk tubes with ornamental tassels or by attaching metal cylinders to the ends of the plaits **(Fig. 10)**.

Fig. 6 Mid twelfth century

Fig. 7 *c.* 1130–*c.* 1160

Fig. 8
c. 1090–1130

Fig. 9 Mid twelfth century

Fig. 10 *c.* 1130–1145

Plantagenet
1154–1399

The Plantagenet period extended over almost two and a half centuries and for the greater part of that time there was little change in the basic style of dress of both sexes, although new ideas continued to appear.

The state of society was still such that women were on the whole much confined to their homes, even ladies of rank being mainly occupied in running their households. A plain kirtle and veil similar to that worn by their servants would probably have been sufficient for daily wear whilst more elaborate costume would be worn for tournaments and hunting. As in previous centuries the quality and style of garments depended more on the rank of the wearer than on fashion. The latest styles worn at Court would only have been copied by those living in London.

Long, full garments were still worn; the close fitting bodices adopted by the minority during the reign of Stephen had disappeared by the beginning of Henry II's reign. The sleeves of the gown were loose and wide at the armhole and tight fitting at the wrist. About the middle of the thirteenth century the super tunic was replaced by the *surcote*, a garment without sleeves. Later a version with sleeves was also worn. Mantles and cloaks now tended to be worn only for travelling and by the nobility on State occasions. Although clothes were plain and simply cut the range of imported materials was increasing. In addition to the usual wool and linen several varieties of silk were in use and fur of many kinds was available for linings and trimmings.

By the beginning of the Plantagenet era women had already ceased to wear long plaits and their hair was once more hidden from public view by a veil, albeit a much smaller one than had hitherto been usual. The "covered up" appearance was enhanced by the adoption of two new styles of headdress, the barbette and wimple, but before long the hair began to be revealed once more, if not directly, then by the invention of headdresses which required an abundance of hair to make them effective.

Loose-flowing hair was still usual for young girls and was also worn in this manner beneath their crowns by queens on State occasions. Light veils might also be worn, but the hair was always visible. Girls are sometimes depicted in manuscripts of the time wearing chaplets of flowers, or metal and jewelled fillets designed to imitate such decorations.

During the second quarter of the fourteenth century notable changes in costume began to take place. The first signs of change had been apparent earlier in the century, but it was in the reign of Edward III that fashion in the sense that we understand it began to develop. Not only was there a fundamental alteration in the shape of clothes, with a pronounced emphasis on the outline of the figure, but also a greater distinction between the dress of men and women, which had hitherto been very similar. Due to more settled conditions and increasing foreign trade a greater variety of expensive fabrics was becoming available to those who could afford them. Decoration was more lavish, with large floral and geometric patterns, heraldic designs and much jewelled embroidery becoming popular.

There was still a great social gulf between the nobility and the rest of the nation, but as the middle classes increased in prosperity they acquired a taste for the luxuries which had formerly been the prerogative of the wealthy. Sumptuary laws were introduced by Edward III in an attempt to curb the expenditure of all classes and indirectly to prevent those in humbler circumstances imitating the fashions of the nobility. Directions were given as to the cost of clothing to be worn by those of different degrees and the amount and type of trimming or jewellery. In spite of these measures the costume became even more elaborate, reaching a peak of extravagance at the end of the period in the reign of Richard II, who was himself fond of fashionable clothes.

Women's clothing was on the whole simpler than that of the men, the main changes and fashion interest being centred on the headdress. The gown, or *cotehardie* as it was now called, became close fitting, with full drapery from the hips. Sleeves were long and tight, necklines low and wide. The sleeveless surcote of the thirteenth century was transformed into the sideless surcote. The bodice portion was cut away at the sides, leaving only a broad band of material or fur encircling the shoulders, with panels down the front and back of the body. These panels were attached to bands below hip level from which hung the full skirt. This surcote was worn over the cotehardie and was one of the most important garments of the late Middle Ages. The simple fitted style of dress served to set off the elaborate headdresses and veils which became increasingly fashionable and varied after 1350.

17

Plantagenet

1 Wimple, barbette and crespine

The fashion for uncovered hair and long plaits which was at its height during the reign of Stephen appeared to decline soon after the middle of the century. Instead, the plaits were coiled over the ears or arranged across the back of the head. The hair was usually covered with the *couvre-chef* which, although quite short, was of the same rectangular or semicircular cut as those worn in the previous period.

During the second half of the twelfth century the *barbette* and the *wimple* were the first distinctive items of headdress to be worn by Englishwomen in addition to the age-old veil and circlet. The barbette, which was supposed to have been introduced by Eleanor of Aquitaine, the wife of Henry II, was a band of linen encircling the face and pinned in position on top of the head. At first, it was worn by royal and noble ladies with the new style of small veil and a crown or coronet (**Fig. 11**) but during the thirteenth century it was adopted by women of all classes. The wimple, which appeared about 1190, was a length of fine linen or silk draped across the throat close beneath the chin, the ends being pinned to the hair on the crown of the head. The wimple was always worn with a veil and sometimes with a circlet also and it remained an important item of headwear for two centuries (**Fig. 12**).

Early in the reign of Henry III the *fillet* became an important part of the headdress. This took the form of a stiffened band of linen or silk which was worn round the head over the barbette. The band varied in width from about one and a half to four inches and the deeper type sometimes had the top covered, thus giving it the appearance of a hat, and was usually rather plain. The open type on the other hand was frequently pleated or *goffered*. When those of royal or noble birth wore their crowns or coronets these were placed on the head outside the fillet, the latter showing above the points of the crown.

Young girls wore the barbette and fillet with flowing hair (**Fig. 17**), but it was more usual for the hair to be braided low across the back of the head or coiled in a large knot at the nape of the neck (**Fig. 13**). Later it was covered with a net known as a *crespine* or *crespinette*. These nets or cauls in many different forms were to be an important part of women's headdress until late in the fifteenth century. They were attached to a band worn round the head, and were very frequently worn in conjunction with the fillet and barbette (**Fig. 15** and **Fig. 16**). The crespine was popular with women in all walks of life and continued to be worn by the working classes until well into the fourteenth century. Those worn by great ladies were made of silk cord studded with jewels or metal at the intersections of the mesh, whilst those of the less wealthy were of coarser material. **Figs 14** and **15** show the crespine worn with the hair dressed in coils over the ears or plaits round the head, styles which became fashionable generally towards the end of the thirteenth century. The fillet tended to become wider at the sides in order to fit over these styles (**Fig. 16**). Before the end of Edward I's reign both the fillet and barbette became considerably narrower (**Fig. 15**).

Fig. 11 1154–1190

Fig. 12 *c.* 1190

Fig. 13 *c.* 1250

Fig. 14 *c.* 1250–1300

Fig. 15 *c.* 1300

Fig. 16 1250–1300

Fig. 17 *c.* 1290

Plantagenet

2 Wimple and hair

In the last decade of the thirteenth century there was a fashion for arranging the hair in plaited coils over the ears, a style which continued to be worn during the reign of Edward II. The crespine, which remained popular, was adapted to cover these side coils by being divided into two sections attached to either side of the headband. It was also still worn in the original fashion to cover the whole of the head.

The wimple, however, continued to be by far the most important article of headwear. At the beginning of the fourteenth century it was frequently worn without the veil in the manner shown in **Fig. 19**, that is, pinned over the coils on either side of the head. When the wimple was worn alone in this way it was often known as the gorget. **Fig. 24** shows a wimple of this type worn with a circlet and veil. The coils of hair may be seen projecting under the latter. Another way of wearing the hair also appeared about this time. From a centre parting the hair was divided and plaited as before, but these braids were now arranged horizontally round the head, the ends being pinned out of sight. A band was sometimes used to keep the hair in place and the wimple was secured underneath the plaits, the bottom edge being usually tucked into the neck of the gown **(Fig. 18)**.

Towards the middle of the fourteenth century women adopted the fashion of wearing the plaits vertically on either side of the face. **Fig. 20** and **Fig. 21** show two methods of arranging the hair in this way. In **Fig. 23** another slight variation of the style appears, with a rare example of the wimple which is wired to stand away from the face and hair. Younger women frequently wore no head covering, but a fillet was sometimes worn to support the plaits **(Fig. 22)**. The cheek pieces visible between the plaits and the face were apparently attached to the fillet, but their purpose is not known.

Fig. 18 Early fourteenth century

Fig. 19 Early fourteenth century

Fig. 20 Mid fourteenth century

Fig. 21 Mid fourteenth century

Fig. 22 Mid fourteenth century

Fig. 23 1330

Fig. 24 1310

Plantagenet

3 Development of the crespine

The fashion for wearing the hair in vertical braids continued until the end of the Plantagenet period and artificial hair was undoubtedly often used. It is highly likely that a headdress such as that illustrated in **Fig. 25** consisting of a gold or silver fillet, often set with jewels, with the cheek pieces and false plaits already attached was made to be placed on the head in one complete piece, the lady's own hair having previously been plaited and coiled over the ears or pinned round the back of the head and covered with the veil. An elaborate version of this headdress was worn by royalty and nobility. It was a development of the crespine or net caul and was the forerunner of the ornate headdresses which were to become so important a part of women's costume in the next century. In the making of these re-markable creations, narrow bands of metal (or metal wire) were formed into flexible or reticu-lated mesh and fashioned into two cylinders which fitted on either side of the head in front of the ears and enclosed the plaits or unbound tresses of hair which were inserted through the open tops. These side cauls were attached to a fillet or coronet which had a semicircular pro-jection on either side forming the tops of the cauls. Jewels were set at the intersections of the mesh and short veils were sometimes worn **(Fig. 27)**. Another variation of the crespine is shown in **Fig. 26**. This was a fairly rare type of headdress which appeared about 1370 and does not seem to have been worn later than about 1400. It took the form of a turban-like cap covering the hair entirely but exposing the ears. These caps would certainly have been lined with silk. When veils were worn they were short and were usually attached either to the top or to the back as shown in the illustration.

About 1370 a new form of veil appeared which was yet another aspect of the fourteenth-century taste for face-framing headdresses. This was a fashion that lasted well into the fifteenth century and was popular with the middle classes and lesser nobility. The veil was semi-circular in shape and was placed on the head with the straight edge framing the face and the curved edge hanging over the shoulders. The front was edged with a ruffle consisting of several layers of goffered or pleated linen which extended from temple to temple **(Fig. 28)**, or down to the jaw line on either side **(Fig. 29)**. Sometimes the curved back edge had a ruffled border to match the front. Occasionally a jewelled fillet was worn beneath the veil, the front being just visible on the brow below the ruffle. Very rarely the ruffle was enclosed in a jewelled net and in this style the fillet encircled the head over the veil **(Fig. 30)**.

Fig. 25 *c.* 1364

Fig. 26 *c.* 1390

Fig. 27 Late fourteenth century

Fig. 28 *c.* 1395

Fig. 29 *c.* 1375

Fig. 30 Late fourteenth century

Plantagenet

4 Veils and hoods

The plain type of veil, either alone or with the wimple, continued to be worn throughout the period, but it eventually became the head attire of the poor and unfashionable, the elderly and widows. The shape was still generally rectangular or semi-circular and was worn either hanging freely or closely draped round the face. **Fig. 31** illustrates the veil arranged in a fold over the front of the head and worn with a wimple covering the chin. The custom of covering the chin with the wimple was one which was prevalent throughout the fourteenth century, particularly towards the end of the period when this particular headdress became the prerogative of widows and women in religious orders. About that time a curious development took place in the wimple. The front portion covering the chin was arranged in vertical pleats and was known as the *barbe* (or *beard*), see page 36 **(Fig. 58** and **Fig. 59)**. This is mentioned by Chaucer in his description of the garb of the Prioress in The Prologue to the *Canterbury Tales*: "Ful semyly hir wympul pynched was . . ."

An interesting variation of the open-fronted veil is shown in **Fig. 35**. In this and similar examples it was worn over a close-fitting hood or coif of linen with a scalloped edge which formed a rectangular frame for the face. Hoods, similar to those worn by men were worn by the upper classes for travelling or when some protection for the head was necessary, otherwise they were a form of headwear which was confined mainly to the middle and lower classes. The usual style of the hood is illustrated in **Fig. 36**. The tubular point known as the *liripipe* was a feature which appeared during the reign of Edward I and was often carried to an exaggerated length of several feet. The hood might be worn open but could also be tied or buttoned under the chin.

Hoods attached to capes or cloaks were also worn in the reign of Edward III, when it was decreed that no woman below a certain rank should go out in a hood furred with other than lambskin or rabbit skin, but those who wore hoods with furred capes might have them of any fur they thought proper. This regulation was made because lower class women were wearing hoods lined or trimmed with a costly fur known as *great vair* or with miniver, in imitation of the wealthy. In a fourteenth-century Romance a queen's riding costume is described as consisting of a short cloak worn over her silken gown with a blue hood decorated with precious stones.

In 1355, at the request of the citizens of London, a statute was introduced by Parliament which ordained that no known prostitutes should wear hoods "except reyed or striped of divers colours, nor furre, but garments reversed or turned the wrong side outward upon paine to forfeit the same". The purpose of this law was not to curb extravagance but to protect the morals of the community by enabling everyone to distinguish prostitutes from respectable women. It was a law which must have been extremely difficult to enforce.

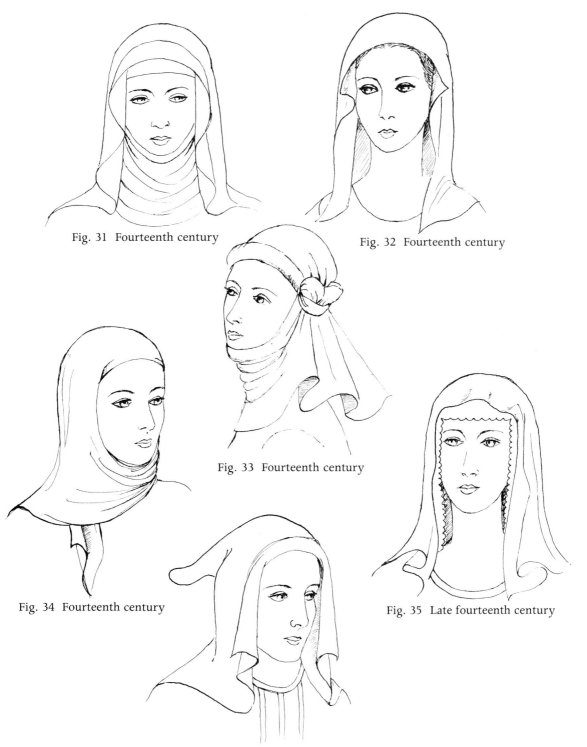

Fig. 31 Fourteenth century

Fig. 32 Fourteenth century

Fig. 33 Fourteenth century

Fig. 34 Fourteenth century

Fig. 35 Late fourteenth century

Fig. 36 Fourteenth century

Lancaster 1399–1461
York 1461–1485

Henry IV 1399–1413   Henry V 1413–1422   Henry VI 1422–1461
Edward IV 1461–1483   Edward V 1483   Richard III 1483–1485

The fashions of the fifteenth century appear to reflect the unsettled conditions of this period, with its long spells of warfare and general unrest. The trend towards constantly changing styles and elaborate clothing, which had become evident in the later Plantagenet era, was continued and intensified. Henry VI introduced further measures intended to curb extravagance and amongst these were regulations concerning the export of gold. In spite of an acute shortage of precious metals in Europe at this time they were being used lavishly for purposes of adornment, especially in the making of women's headdresses.

Apart from the headdresses, women's costume continued to be comparatively simple, showing fewer changes and variations than that of the men. The silhouette was becoming longer, with a high waistline and small bosom. It was fashionable to stand or walk with the hips thrust forward so that the figure profile with skirts trailing behind presented a graceful curve surmounted by the elaborate headdress. About 1400 the *houppelande* was adopted by women. This garment had been a masculine fashion for about 20 years and, at first, the version worn by women was very similar. Its chief characteristic was extreme fullness, which was gathered in at the waist by a belt and fell in close deep folds to the feet, sometimes forming a train. The sleeves were also long and full. The neckline was at first very high but within a few years a broad flat collar had become usual. By 1440 the neck had become V-shaped with revers, the point of the V extending to the belt. About this time the houppelande became known as the gown, the original gown or kirtle being worn as an undergown, its neckline or sleeves being sometimes visible. The cote-hardie and the sideless surcote were still part of the costume, but the former was gradually superseded by the houppelande and the latter was usually worn only on ceremonial occasions.

By about 1450–1460 the gown had developed a tight-fitting bodice and sleeves, with the V-shaped neckline becoming very wide. The skirt was still very full and long, especially at the back, but was now fitted over the hips. Later the neckline became more rounded and was edged with a band of fur or other material contrasting with the gown. Fine white material was often used to fill in the V necklines and very elaborate necklaces were worn with both styles.

Throughout the whole of this period the hair was completely hidden from sight although, as before, young girls were often excepted from this rule. Much ingenuity and skilled craftsmanship was expended on the fantastic headdresses which must have been extremely inconvenient and uncomfortable to wear. It is probable that the more exaggerated examples were only worn on special occasions and that modified versions were usual for everyday wear. Veils and hoods were the normal wear for working women and for many middle class women living in the country. Margaret Paston, writing to her husband from her home in Norwich in 1449, requested him to bring her a yard of black broadcloth to make a hood, and in 1463 she wrote of her intention to use some satin which he had given her for a hood to make a collar for a new gown.

Lancaster

1 Reticulated and turban headdress

The headdress styles of this period fall into four main categories: the reticulated, the horned, the heart shaped and the turban. As will be seen from the illustrations on the opposite and following pages the first group, after a short spell of development along distinctive lines, merged into the second and third groups. The reticulated headdresses were really variations on the crespine and the cylindrical cauls of the previous period and had been worn by highly fashionable ladies during the last years of the fourteenth century. Instead of the cylindrical form, numerous rounded or squarish box-like shapes were common and were attached, as before, to a circlet or coronet. At first the cauls were worn above the ears but very soon they became larger, covering the ears completely. The hair was now hidden by the metal mesh which covered the whole head (**Fig. 37** and **Fig. 39A**) and the tightly coiled plaits were enclosed in the cauls. The style shown in **Fig. 37** was always worn with a veil falling to the shoulders. A short veil might also be attached when the cauls were worn with a crown or coronet (**Fig. 39**) or with the elaborate padded roll shown in **Fig. 38**. Turban-style headdresses made an appearance early in this period but did not become popular until the middle of the century. These padded rolls of silk or velvet were decorated with pearls and jewels and a veil was usually draped over the top, either flowing loose or swathed round the chin (**Fig. 40**). **Fig. 41** shows an example of the reticulated headdress with the later development of the large cauls covering the ears.

Fig. 37 1404

Fig. 38 1405

Fig. 39a

Fig. 39 1410

Fig. 41a

Fig. 40 c. 1410

Fig. 41 c. 1412

Lancaster

2 Horned headdress

During the reign of Henry V the large box-like cauls reached their maximum size and width (**Fig. 42** and **Fig. 43**) and the first examples of the horned headdress appeared. **Fig. 44** shows an elaborate example of what may be considered a transitional style. The cauls have reached extremely large proportions and support wide branching wires, thus achieving the horned appearance. A voluminous rectangular veil with a slightly curved edge is arranged over this wire framework. It was not unusual during the fifteenth century for coronets such as the one shown here to be shaped to fit between the horns of the headdress and to curve down the back of the head. They were probably made to fit over metal circlets which formed part of the underlying structure of the headdress, the veils, when worn, being caught between the two sections. **Fig. 45** shows the further development of the horned headdress in which the horns were formed of padded material. The side cauls went quickly out of fashion towards the end of Henry V's reign and the horns became an integral part of the headdress. The metal mesh which had formed the framework for the cauls was now frequently used as a decorative covering for the horned and heart-shaped headwear.

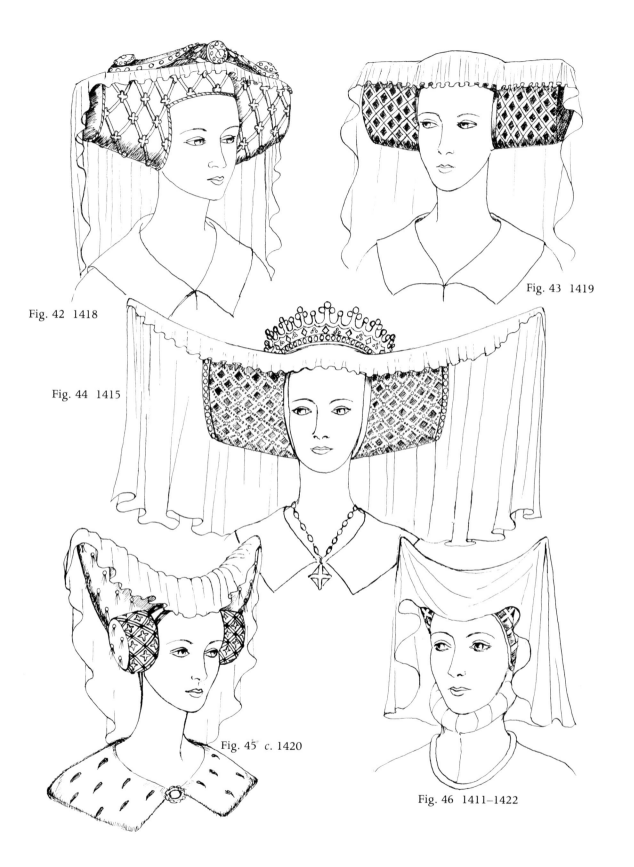

Fig. 42 1418

Fig. 43 1419

Fig. 44 1415

Fig. 45 *c.* 1420

Fig. 46 1411–1422

3 Heart-shaped and turban headdress

The illustrations show some further examples of the headdresses of this period. As time went on the horned formation became less wide and the side pieces, or templers as they were sometimes called, gradually rose from the almost horizontal position shown in **Fig. 47** to the nearly vertical, thus becoming heart-shaped **(Fig. 48)**. Between these two, many slight variations occurred. Elaborate versions of the heart-shaped headdress enclosed in heavy goldsmith's work and set with precious stones were worn for ceremonial occasions **(Fig. 49)**, but as a rule they were formed of rich fabrics which were either encased in a light-weight gold mesh or were decorated with needlework or jewels. They were certainly regarded as heirlooms by the women of the period, who occasionally mentioned them in their wills. The circular or rectangular veils were either very short or just below shoulder length.

Fig. 50 and **Fig. 51** show two further variations of the heart-shaped headdress. In both cases the lower portion was covered with mesh and surmounted by a padded roll of fabric sewn with jewels. The shaped pieces of fabric hanging from the top of the example in **Fig. 51** and the long tail or liripipe were copied from the *chaperone*, a fashionable fifteenth-century masculine headdress.

The turban-style headdress was popular over a considerable period; instances of its use may be found throughout the fifteenth century. It was probably Turkish in inspiration for it was after the capture of Constantinople in 1453 that this fashion reached its peak. The large draped style shown in **Fig. 52** appeared quite frequently. It was apparently of light construction and probably consisted of a wire framework with silk or fine linen gathered over it. Other turban styles were made of rich fabric decorated all over with jewels or sometimes a single large jewel was placed in front. Star and crescent-shaped ornaments were a further indication of the Turkish origin of this type of headdress.

Fig. 47 *c.* 1430

Fig. 48 *c.* 1455

Fig. 49 *c.* 1440

Fig. 50 *c.* 1445

Fig. 51 *c.* 1450–*c.* 1460

Fig. 52 *c.* 1455

York

4 Hennin and butterfly headdress

There seems to be little evidence that the steeple headdress so closely associated in many people's minds with the costume of the Middle Ages was ever worn to any extent in England. It was extremely fashionable in Flanders and France where it first appeared about 1430, and it seems to have been introduced into England around the middle of the century, but it is usually associated with the early Yorkist period. It is always called the *hennin*, a term whose real meaning remains obscure. One theory is that it was a satirical or insulting word applied to horned headdresses generally, another that it was so-called because it was invented by a certain Dame de Henin in imitation of a similar Eastern headdress. Whatever its origin it would appear to have been a natural development of the previously fashionable horned headdress; the two horns having become higher and closer until finally they became one.

The hennin consisted of a cone shape made of rich fabric either stiffened with wire or smoothly padded. In the English version the point of the cone was omitted and the top was flattened, the total height of the headdress being not more than about nine inches, in contrast to the two or three feet attained by the Continental examples. Placed on the head at an angle of about 40 degrees the hennin always showed a rounded or V-shaped loop in the centre front. This frontlet was made of black material and its purpose, apart from being decorative, was probably to enable the wearer to adjust the headdress as its weight and the angle must have exercised a considerable backward pull. A sumptuary law which was in force throughout this period permitted only the wives and daughters of persons having possessions of the yearly value of £10 or more to use and wear frontlets of black velvet. The weight must have been increased by the large transparent veils which were either attached to the top of the hennin or draped all over and frequently reaching the ground. Earlier examples were elaborately wired out and some-times narrow lengths were draped beneath the chin.

Young girls sometimes wore this headdress without a veil and with their hair flowing loosely behind, but other women continued the custom of hiding the hair completely, even pursuing the ideal of a high bare forehead to the extent of plucking and shaving the hair from the temples and also from the nape of the neck, whilst eyebrows were trimmed to a fine line.

About 1470 a broad band of black material was attached to the base of the hennin across the front from side to side of the head and the ends hung down to shoulder level or below **(Fig. 53)**.

A headdress which was a modified version of the hennin, and was certainly more popular with Englishwomen, made its appearance early in the reign of Edward IV and continued to be worn by the fashion conscious until well into the early Tudor period. This headdress, often called the *butterfly*, consisted of a cap resembling an inverted flower pot, although very frequently the top and base were of equal circumference. It was made of fabric which was either richly patterned or embroidered. At first the cap was placed on the head at a similar angle to that of the original hennin, but it soon became fashionable to set it far back so that it was in an almost horizontal position. Worn in this way a certain amount of hair became visible, although the bare look was still sought after. The arrangement of the transparent veil was an interesting and important feature of this headdress. Sometimes it was folded and pinned to the centre front in the way shown in **Fig. 57** but more often it was draped over two or three fine wires which radiated from the centre front of the cap. In many cases the frontal loop was still retained often forming an exaggerated V shape. In addition a strip of veiling similar to the band on the hennin was a feature of many butterfly headdresses. This front band formed an important part of another headdress which was simply a truncated version of the hennin and was the forerunner of the hoods of the Tudor period **(Fig. 55)**.

The turban and heart-shaped styles in various forms were still worn in this period. **Fig. 54** shows an elaborate version of the latter worn at the new fashionable angle and having a shaped metal band supporting a coronet.

Fig. 53 1460–1470

Fig. 54 1475

Fig. 55 1485

Fig. 56 1480

Fig. 57 1484

Lancaster and York

5 Fifteenth-century miscellaneous headwear

The veil and the wimple with the pleated linen bib or *barbe* was the accepted form of headwear for widows and women in religious orders throughout the fifteenth century. Although remaining basically the same during this time the headdress could be varied to suit individual taste or could be adapted slightly to conform with prevailing fashions. Veils, arranged in various ways, were rectangular or semi-circular in shape and often had pleated or scalloped edges. As with other forms of headdress, coronets might be worn on State occasions by those of noble rank. Although veils continued to be worn by many widows until well into the seventeenth century, the wimple and barbe had died out by the beginning of the sixteenth century except for Court mourning. A curious ordinance intended to govern the apparel to be worn at times of Court mourning was drawn up by Margaret, Countess of Richmond, a few years after her son, Henry VII, came to the throne. She specified the clothing—much of it in a style fast going out of fashion—to be worn by people of different ranks, beginning with the Queen. The ladies were directed to wear hoods with tippets (a long narrow tail or tube similar to the liripipe) varying in length according to the rank of the wearer, the Queen having the longest, and "everyone not beying under the degree of baronesse, to wear a barbe above the chynne, and all other as knyghtes wiefes, to wear it under there throte, and other gentlewomen beneath the throte roll".

The custom of wearing the hair flowing loose, which had been usual amongst young girls since Saxon times, was continued throughout the Middle Ages. Brides and queens at their coronation and perhaps on certain State occasions also wore their hair in this manner. **Fig. 60** illustrates a girl wearing a circlet with a V-shaped loop similar to those on the fashionable headdresses of the Yorkist period. This triangular decoration may be the "beake" which seems to have been a rare fashion and was expressly forbidden by Margaret of Richmond in her regulation concerning Court mourning. She referred to it as "deformitie".

Fig. 61 illustrates an example of the kind of headcovering which might have been worn by any poor woman. A piece of material draped round the head was surmounted by an old hat of the type worn by men during this period. A wooden spoon was stuck in the band.

Fig. 58 1425

Fig. 59 1460

Fig. 60 1480

Fig. 61 1480

Fig. 62 1460

Tudor
1485–1558

The style of costume worn during the reign of Henry VII is transitional between that of the medieval period and that which, usually thought of as typically Tudor, is familiar from the portraits of Henry VIII and his contemporaries. As far as women's dress was concerned, this is largely true as there were few distinctive changes to be seen until almost the end of the century.

The gown styles of the latter part of the Yorkist period remained fashionable for some time, but about 1495 a new style appeared. This had a close-fitting bodice with a square neck, above which appeared the top of the kirtle or the folds of the neckerchief. Sometimes the bodice was laced across a wide V opening down the front to below the waistline. The sleeves were loose and very wide at the wrist and turned back to form a cuff. The skirt was full and very long, forming a train behind. This train was sometimes carried over the arm or was turned up behind and fastened to the waist in order to show a lining of contrasting material or fur. Elaborate girdles with hanging ends in front were always worn. The headdresses were variations on the bonnet style or the hood developing about 1500 into the exclusively English *gable* hood, so called from its resemblance to a roof. This headdress was perhaps the most distinctive feature of women's dress throughout the first 40 years of the sixteenth century.

The Tudor period was one of great ostentation and extravagance in dress. Henry VIII was extremely fond of clothes and finery, and all those who had sufficient wealth, including the merchant class were dressed in the most lavish manner. Women's costume began to lose the simplicity and elegance it had retained for centuries and rivalled that of the men in richness and elaboration. The luxurious materials available, the costly fabrics and fur, thick embroidery and heavy jewellery all helped to create an effect of solidity and stiffness. From about 1525 it became increasingly fashionable to discard the gown and wear the kirtle alone and in consequence it became much more elaborate. The skirt was a smooth cone shape, without folds or drapery, achieved by the use of a stiff petticoat and later by the Spanish farthingale which was formed by a series of hoops attached to an underskirt. The skirt of the kirtle was often open down the front, revealing an underskirt of contrasting material. The bodice was stiff from neckline to waist, with a very wide, square neck curving upwards slightly in the centre front but forming a V at the back. The neck edge was bordered with lace and jewels and a double necklace with a heavy pendant was always worn. Sometimes the chemise had a stand-up collar which was visible above the neck of the kirtle, or a separate fill-in known as a partlet was worn. An alternative neckline became fashionable after 1535. This was a low stand-up or *Medici* collar, open in front to reveal either a short necklace or the chemise collar edged with a frill. The sleeves were a remarkable feature and were of two kinds. The first consisted of two parts, an oversleeve and an undersleeve. The oversleeve was tight fitting round the upper arm, expanding at the elbow into a bell shape which was turned back to form an enormous cuff of fur or contrasting material. The undersleeves, which were detachable, were either fairly close fitting or were shaped in a great curve from wrist to elbow. Both types were often slashed and the chemise sleeve pulled through to form puffs. The other kind of sleeve was very full, the seams being either trimmed with embroidery or left open and caught together at intervals with jewelled fastenings. The chemise sleeve was pulled out in puffs through the openings. The frilled cuffs of the chemise were always visible at the wrists in both types of sleeve.

During the short reigns of Edward VI and Mary I few changes in costume occurred. Spanish influence was becoming more pronounced in the increasing stiffness and formality of the clothes. The farthingale skirt was now universally worn except by poorer women. The bodice was held rigid by stays of wood or whalebone, the waistline being low and pointed in front. A coat-like garment or over-gown, a new style of tight-fitting sleeve with a large puff at the shoulder and the English version of the French hood were the only new fashions to be introduced during those 11 years.

Tudor

1 Early hood headdress

Although the headdresses of the previous period continued to be worn for a few years they were soon completely superseded by the hood, which in a variety of forms became fashionable wear for more than 60 years and was still worn by many until the beginning of the seventeenth century.

In its earliest form, with a round crown and front band with long side pieces, it was a direct development of the truncated form of the hennin (**Fig. 63**). The crown was made in sections and trimmed with contrasting bands of material. This style is sometimes called the *bonnet* headdress. A second type of hood consisted of a semicircular piece of heavy fabric lined with a contrasting colour and attached to an undercap. The straight edge of the semicircle was placed across the front of the head and folded back to show the lining and sometimes the undercap as well. This edge was often shaped into a curve. The remainder of the material hung down the back in folds to below shoulder level but was usually slit on either side, the front pieces thus forming lappets (**Fig. 64**). The undercap, made of linen, velvet or gauze, and the edges of the hood and slits were sometimes embroidered or jewelled. These two types of hood, both of Franco-Flemish origin, developed a number of variations during the closing years of the fifteenth century, and finally the styles became merged into the truly English fashion of the gable or pedimental headdress. The forehead loop was still retained in many cases, but the fashion died out during the early years of the sixteenth century as the centre front of the hood acquired the gabled appearance.

Figs 65 and **66** illustrate two of the transitional versions of the hood which were worn by the middle classes. **Fig. 65** shows the semi-circular draped form allied to a flattened crown or caul, whilst a separate front band replaces the turned back fold. This band was ornamented with embroidery or jewels or might even be made of fur. The style was also associated with the gabled front.

In **Fig. 66** the caul was very rounded and may even have been slightly padded and was possibly incorporated into the undercap. The top was wired or stiffened to form a horizontal line along the top of the head from front to back and even projected for two or three inches beyond the crown. The material which formed the hood was draped over this structure and may have been of a light-weight or even transparent nature. The front band consisted of a separate piece, either plain or gable-shaped and may have been of heavier fabric than that used for the main part of the headdress. A drawing by Hans Holbein dated 1540 shows a middle-class English woman wearing a headdress of similar construction.

Fig. 67 shows an elaborate early example of the gable headdress which was worn by royalty and nobility. The roof-like construction of the crown may be seen here in conjunction with the sharply arched front which gives the headdress its name. This frontal framework was probably made of light metal, wire or stiff fabric covered with dark material similar to that used for the rest of the headdress and was then faced with jewelled embroidery. Another band of jewelled decoration was placed over the head behind the arched frontlet and hung down on either side. At the back the folds of the material hung down almost to the wearer's waist.

The hood was lined with a light colour and the hair, with a centre parting, was allowed to show to a limited extent. It was probably braided or coiled at the back, but there is evidence that it may sometimes have been worn loose.

Widows and elderly women continued to wear the wimple with the gable hood, and the pleated barbe was still favoured as a sign of mourning. Those in religious orders also continued to wear it with the wimple and a plain veil.

A plain hood of Flemish origin with the front edge lightly stiffened to form a small dip in the centre was sometimes adopted by middle class women. It was made either of white linen or, as in the case of the other types of hood in heavier dark material. This form of hood eventually developed into the style well known for its association with Mary, Queen of Scots.

Fig. 63 *c.* 1490

Fig. 64 *c.* 1495

Fig. 65 1519

Fig. 66 *c.* 1517

Fig. 67 *c.* 1501

Tudor

2 Gable hoods

In the course of the 1520's the gable headdress underwent a number of changes. The front lappets, which had previously hung down on either side of the face (**Fig. 68**) now tended to be turned up about level with the ears and the ends fastened to the crown of the hood. These lappets and the front portion of the hood over the top of the head were often made of rich fabric embroidered or jewelled (**Fig. 70**).

The back drape was replaced by two broad strips of double material and one or both of these might also be turned up and pinned to the top (**Fig. 71**). These strips were either attached to the top of the gable or, as shown in **Fig. 69**, to the base of the diamond-shaped caul. The stiffened linen undercap was an important part of the headdress for it formed a base for the whole structure, including the jewelled front. The sides were shaped to curve in to the cheeks and were visible curling outwards at the jawline. The sides of the undercap became shorter and narrower during the 1520's (compare **Fig. 68** with **Figs 70** and **71**). The cap was sometimes fastened under the chin with a narrow white band. The hair was completely hidden, the space between the forehead and the gable front being filled with two silk-covered pads which overlapped in the centre. These pads or rolls were a later development of an earlier practice of wearing the hair in this manner. It was divided into two swathes or braids bound spirally with ribbon and these were crossed on the brow to fill the gap formed by the gable. Subsequently the silk pads were always striped in semblance of the ribbon.

The gable hood continued to be worn by the middle and lower classes and especially by older women until at least the middle of the century.

Fig. 68 *c.* 1525

Fig. 69 *c.* 1530

Fig. 70 *c.* 1540

Fig. 71 *c.* 1540

Tudor

3 French hoods

The French hood became fashionable in the 1520's and, gradually superseding the gable, it remained high fashion for at least 40 years and continued to be worn by many until the beginning of the seventeenth century. It was made on a stiffened or wired foundation of curved horseshoe shape worn far back on the head, exposing a good deal of centre-parted hair. The embroidered or pleated edge of the undercap was revealed round the front of the headdress. Behind this edge the front portion of the hood consisted of a band of velvet or satin about two to three inches wide. The usual colours were black, red or white, and later two bands of colour were sometimes used, for example a red upper band and a white lower band. The back was almost always of black material, probably velvet, and a single hanging piece of double fabric, either plain or pleated, replaced the two flaps which had characterized the gable hood (**Figs 73** and **74**).

The jewelled borders encircling the front edge and the crown of the hood were known as the upper and nether *billiments* or *habillements*. Made of pearls and precious or semi-precious stones set in gold, these billiments often matched the borders of the low, square necklines of the gowns and sometimes they matched girdles and necklaces also. At her trial in 1553 Lady Jane Grey wore a black satin hood trimmed with jet. As a general rule the jewels of the upper billiment were attached to a foundation of black velvet matching the back fall and those of the lower billiment were on a similar foundation which matched the colour of the hood front. These edges of velvet or other material sometimes had no jewelled decoration. Two portraits of Margaret of Scotland, sister of Henry VIII, show her wearing hoods without jewels. **Fig. 72**, taken from a portrait of one of the daughters of Sir Thomas More, shows an English version of the French hood. The crown is low and the front is reminiscent of the gable style. In the original painting a narrow pink velvet border is just visible between the jewelled front of the hood and the embroidered edge of the white undercap. The chin band securing the undercap was still worn in many cases. It is possible that when no chin band was worn the undercap was dispensed with and the pleated edging was attached to the hood itself.

Another English variation of the hood (**Fig. 75**) had an upper billiment only and a deep frontlet of black velvet attached to the front edge. Sometimes this frontlet had a downward dip in the centre from front to back.

During the reigns of Edward VI and Mary I the French hood became generally popular and its shape altered slightly. The front edge was now wired in such a manner as to curve forward on either side of the face touching the cheeks or the temples, and the crown was somewhat higher (**Fig. 77**). Mary I, both as Princess and Queen, favoured a style of hood with a flatter crown (**Fig. 76**), but this shape does not appear to have been generally adopted.

The back flap of the hood was sometimes turned up and placed across the top of the head with the end projecting over the forehead to shade the complexion from the sun. This arrangement was known as a *bongrace*. It was also worn as a separate item, being a stiffened ablong piece of material pinned over the hood or coif with one end over the forehead and the other hanging down the back. After about 1540 fashionable women wore their hair waved or puffed at the temples.

Fig. 72 1527

Fig. 73 c. 1539

Fig. 74 c. 1530

Fig. 75 1541

Fig. 76 c. 1554

Fig. 77 c. 1555

Tudor

4 Caps and hats

An undercap similar to that shown in **Fig. 79** was always worn under hats and caps. It was made of white linen, or sometimes of coloured velvet or other material and was wired to keep its shape, and secured by a white strap beneath the chin. A band or frontlet of matching material was worn round the front of the head, just showing beneath the cap. The edge of the frontlet might be embroidered or goffered. A pin secured the cap to the hair and frontlet when no chin band was used. The piece of material swathed round the head and knotted at the back may have been a foundation to which the overcap or hat was pinned.

When the undercap was worn with the French hood the curve of the front was adapted to follow the fashionable shape. The frontlet was omitted and instead the edge of the cap itself was embroidered or pleated and showed all round the front of the hood.

Hats were uncommon during this period, but when worn they were of the flat, halo-brimmed type similar to that worn by men, but whereas the latter wore them at an angle women invariably wore them straight with a slightly backward tilt. These hats were made of velvet and according to the wealth of the wearer would be decorated with gold ornaments, jewels and enamelled tags or *aiglettes*, even the feathers being hung with pearls. The example shown in **Fig. 83** was worn by Catherine Parr, sixth wife of Henry VIII. The white satin undercap, edged with pearls, and the pleated frontlet are plainly visible. Henry's sister Mary, wore a jewelled cap with a red velvet hat for her first meeting with her husband Louis XIII in 1514.

The *lettice* cap **(Fig. 78)** was made of a fur of this name which resembled ermine. It was triangular in shape, with the front edge curved back to show the hair and coming forward on each side of the face. It later became smaller, with shorter side pieces, and was worn with an undercap or frontlet. It was worn chiefly during the second quarter of the century but was men-tioned by Stubbes, the Puritan writer, as late as 1583.

The caps shown in **Figs 81** and **82** were also worn chiefly during the same period, and were white or light in colour. The style in **Fig. 81** tended to become smaller in size later in the period.

An article known as a muffler appeared at some time towards the middle of the century. It would appear to have been worn at first by the upper classes but during the Elizabethan period it was a middle-class fashion. Mufflers of velvet and sable were among the articles belonging to the Royal Wardrobe which Lady Jane Grey had to return when she was imprisoned in 1553. Mufflers are described on page 53.

Fig. 78 *c.* 1530

Fig. 79 *c.* 1540

Fig. 80 *c.* 1536

Fig. 81 *c.* 1535

Fig. 82 *c.* 1540

Fig. 83 *c.* 1545

Elizabethan
1558–1603

In the dress of both sexes the Elizabethan age was perhaps the most extravagant in English history, particularly during the last 25 years of the Queen's reign. Like her father, Elizabeth was extremely fond of clothes and jewels and with advancing years she indulged her taste to an increasing extent. At her death her wardrobe was reputed to have contained at least a thousand dresses and numerous wigs. The Court and those who could afford to do so dressed with equal lavishness. If the evidence of a foreign visitor of the time is to be believed, rich clothes were also worn by many who could ill afford them. Frederick, Duke of Würtemburg, commented on the exceedingly fine clothes of the Englishwomen and added that many did not hesitate to wear velvet in the streets, whilst at home they had not a piece of dry bread.

Until about 1580 the costume remained similar to that of the previous period, the chief variation occurring in the style of the sleeves. The very wide sleeve went out of fashion in the early years of the reign, but the tight-fitting style with a shoulder puff remained popular, as did the full bishop sleeve with the addition of padded wings or rolls projecting from the shoulders. Since the reign of Edward VI the bodice and skirt had been made separately; the waist of the former continued to be shaped to a point in front, while the skirt or kirtle, as it was now called, was still supported by the Spanish farthingale. The bodice might have a high neck and be fastened up the front but the low square neck also continued in fashion and was filled in as before by the top of the chemise or by a partlet of decorative or embroidered material finished with a high collar or with a ruff, the characteristic feature of Elizabethan dress. With the introduction of starch in the early 1560's the ruff grew both in size and in popularity.

In 1580 a new style of bodice and the French "roll" farthingale were introduced and adopted by the fashionable. It was from this time that the silhouette of the wealthy Elizabethan women took on the fantastic appearance familiar from numerous portraits of the Queen. The figure, encased in the long narrow bodice with the flat triangular stomacher stiffened and encrusted with jewels, seemed pinched between the wide hips and the huge padded *trunk* sleeves. The head was framed by the large ruff which was either circular, completely enclosing the neck, or fan shaped, rising from the sides and back of the low neck line. An upstanding, wired lace collar called a *rebato* was also fashionable from this time. The hair was dressed high and was frizzed and curled in order to give the head some importance against the great ruffs and collars. This period was a significant one in the history of headdress for two reasons. It was during the later years of Elizabeth's reign that for the first time in England younger married women went about with their hair uncovered wearing simply jewelled ornaments or little net cauls; hitherto it had been quite usual for unmarried girls to expose their hair but for a married woman to do so was a breach of age old custom. The second notable development in the headwear of this period was the increasing popularity of hats, especially among the middle classes, towards the end of the century. The hats were of many different materials because those of felt and especially beaver had to be imported from France and the Netherlands and were consequently very expensive. Among the many refugees who came to England in the sixteenth century were groups of French and Dutch hatmakers. A number of these settled in Southwark and Bermondsey in 1567, and within a few years felt hats were being widely worn by English men. It is probable that the material was not at first so popular with women, who seemed to prefer softer fabrics. In 1599 a foreign visitor remarked that English burghers' wives usually wore high hats covered with velvet or silk. Hat bands were extremely important and the making of these was apparently a separate trade.

Elizabethan

1 Hair and headdress

The centre parted hair waved or rolled smoothly back at the temples which had become fashionable in the 1540's continued to be worn in this manner during the early years of Elizabeth's reign. Frizzing and close curls were also common, with the back hair enclosed in a cap or caul of reticulated goldsmith's work set with pearls and precious stones and lined with coloured silk or cloth of gold or silver. These cauls were also made in net mesh of gold, silver or silk thread and occasionally of hair—"Two cowls, the one of gold, the other of silver, knytt" were among the New Year gifts to the Queen in 1561–62. **Fig. 84** shows a caul edged with pearls and a jewelled upper billiment. A popular hairstyle during the first 15 or 20 years of this period is shown in **Fig. 85.** The hair was parted in the centre and rolled smoothly back, probably over pads. The same style is shown with a cap of figured gold brocade **(Fig. 89)** and a plain black hood **(Fig. 86)**.

In the 1570's and 1580's the hair was drawn up from the forehead without a parting and arranged over larger pads or wire frames to a greater height and width, with a downward curve in the centre front giving a heart-shaped appearance. A similarly shaped hair line was considered beautiful and hairs were probably plucked from the forehead to achieve the required shape where it did not occur naturally; or small flat curls were arranged in the appropriate formation **(Fig. 87)**.

During this period it became customary for young women both married and unmarried to wear no head covering even out of doors. Cauls and ornaments were the chief decoration. The back hair was in all cases plaited and coiled in a bun behind the head. Throughout Elizabeth's reign the ideal hair was considered to be fair or red in colour and preferably naturally curly. This was probably because the Queen herself had red-gold hair of which she was said to be very proud. In 1564 Sir James Melville, the Scottish emissary, described her hair as being "more reddish than yellow and curled in appearance naturally". **Fig. 88** is taken from a portrait of the Queen and shows her wearing a veil with an upper billiment as a hair ornament. Veils of transparent material could be either small or large and were sometimes sewn with jewels or spangles. Head rails, much favoured by Queen Elizabeth, were veils which were attached to the shoulders and wired to form a curved shape behind the head.

Fig. 84 1570

Fig. 85 *c.* 1560

Fig. 86 1578

Fig. 87 1589

Fig. 88 1575

Fig. 89 *c.* 1580

Elizabethan

2 Hair and headdress

The heart-shaped arrangement of the hair over wire frames or pads which was fashionable during the 1570's and 1580's continued to be popular until the end of the century, but after 1590 the tendency was for the central dip to disappear and by 1600 curls and frizzing were less usual, the hair being brushed into a high oval shape.

In 1583 Philip Stubbes, in his *Anatomie of Abuses*, launched a tirade against women's fashionable hairstyles "which, of force, must be curled, frizled and crisped, laid out in wreaths and borders, from one ear to another, and, lest it should fall down it is underpropped with forks, wires, and I cannot tell what. . . ." These hairstyles required a good deal of thick hair to achieve the right effect and Stubbes describes the lengths to which women would go to augment their own, dying horsehair or cutting off the fair hair of children, enticing them and bribing them with pennies.

Wigs became fashionable in the last quarter of the century, being first introduced into England about 1572. Queen Elizabeth had a large collection and favoured tightly curled hair which was invariably reddish in colour. A warrant signed by the Queen in 1602 ordered payment to be made to her silkwoman "for six heads of heare, twelve yards of heare curle, and one hundred devises made of heare". **Fig. 96** shows a wig made of strands of hair twisted vertically.

It was customary to use dye at this period and one recipe to make hair "of a faire yellowe or golden colour" consisted of "the last water that is drawn from honie being of a deep red colour, which performeth the same excellently".

Jewels were frequently worn in the hair or wigs during the latter part of the period. Quite large heavy pendants consisting of stones set in gold, as well as smaller brooch type ornaments and pear-shaped pearls were attached to wire or pins and secured to the hair supports or wig foundation. The wearing of these hair *bodkins* was not confined to the wealthy. **Fig. 94** shows a

pendant of amethyst drops set in enamelled gold, intended for a well-to-do woman of middle class. **Fig. 92** shows a hair ornament formed of jewelled initials. An upper billiment or border similar to that which decorated the crown of the French hood was popular as a *head-tire*, as they were now called, and appeared as an edging to the high crest of hair (**Figs 91** and **95**). It either formed part of a small cap, caul or band fitting over the coil of hair at the back or it was simply the back portion of the French hood complete with the black velvet hanging flap. Jewelled ornaments were sometimes placed at the back of the head (**Fig. 93**). Among the many jewels given to Queen Elizabeth each New Year were "a carkenet, upper and nether habilliment of Christalles", "a border of bewegels and seed pearls very smalle" and several "attires for the head" one of which is described as containing seven pieces of gold in various designs garnished with small diamonds, rubies, pearls and opals. Feathers also became popular hair ornaments towards the end of the century. In 1599 Thomas Platter, a foreign visitor, described the Queen as wearing a gown of pure white satin gold-embroidered with a whole bird of paradise for a hear-tire set forward on her head and studded with costly jewels.

Hair laces to bind the hair both at night and during the day are referred to in contemporary literature, but there seems to be no evidence to show exactly how they were used.

The hair was combed with ivory or boxwood combs which were cleaned with special comb brushes or quills. A "combing cloth" was worn to protect the clothing from fallen hairs.

Fig. 90 *c.* 1595–1600

Fig. 91 1600

Fig. 92

Fig. 93 *c.* 1585

Fig. 94

Fig. 95 1593

Fig. 96 1600

Elizabethan

3 Coifs

The coif was a close-fitting cap which was worn at night and for indoor day wear or as a foundation for hoods and hats. It was made in one piece with a seam along the top of the head. The front edge was either straight **(Fig. 99)** or, more fashionably, was cut to a point or curve over the forehead and back from the temples to allow for the rolls of hair **(Fig. 97)**. The forehead cloth was a triangular piece of material matching the coif, which was worn over the front of the head with the point either to the front or to the back, generally the latter, and tied under the chin or at the back of the neck **(Fig. 98)**. The purpose of these cloths is not really understood, but they were worn during illness and at night. The coifs were made of plain linen or fustian (a mixture of cotton and wool with a silky finish) for night wear, but for day time they were decorated with cut work or black work and many were embroidered with coloured silks, gold or silver metal thread and spangles in the beautiful designs so widely used on all articles during the latter part of the sixteenth century. All-over patterns were usual and flower designs were especially popular, although other motifs such as birds, animals and insects were also used. In 1561–62 one of the New Year gifts to the Queen was "a cawle and three forehead cloths of cameryck (cambric) netted with gold". In 1577–78 she received "a night coyf of cameryck cutworke and spangills with a forehead cloth" and again the following year "a night coyf of white cypress flourished over with silver", and "a coyf and forehead cloth of black edged with a small bone lace of gold and roses of gold and silk". **Fig. 100** shows a decorative form of forehead cloth worn with an undercap of fine lawn and a plain black hood wired to the popular heart shape. This style of cap, which hid the hair completely, was favoured by elderly women.

Fig. 101 shows a middle-class woman wearing a coif and hat with a muffler. This was a kind of scarf or half-handkerchief which covered the lower part of the face and was fastened behind the head. It was probably intended as a protection in winter.

Fig. 98 Last quarter of sixteenth century

Fig. 97 Last quarter of sixteenth century

Fig. 99
Last quarter of
sixteenth century

Fig. 100 1590

Fig. 101 1574

Elizabethan

4 Hats

During the first 20 years or so of Elizabeth's reign middle-class women continued to wear lettice caps and gable or French hoods. The beret types of cap worn over an undercap as illustrated on page 45, were not seen after about 1560, but in the course of the period hats in imitation of those worn by men became gradually more and more fashionable amongst all classes. In 1575 a foreign visitor commented that married women wore hats both indoors and out, but younger unmarried women went about bareheaded.

Fig. 102 shows a type of flat bonnet known as a *Taffeta Pipkin* which was popular from the earliest years of the reign until about 1595. It was worn over a caul or net and, as its name implies, was made of taffeta stiffened with paper, buckram or starch. The crown was pleated and the narrow brim could be either straight or curved. Feathers, either long and drooping sideways or set upright in short tufts were often used as trimming in addition to jewels and buttons. The *court bonnet* **(Fig. 104)** was a small brimless cap made of velvet, also trimmed with jewels and buttons, which was fashionable during the same period as the Taffeta Pipkin. Although white feathers were usual, red ones or a combination of red and white were also popular for these small caps. When Queen Elizabeth visited Cambridge in 1564 she was described as wearing a caul set with pearls and precious stones and "a hat that was spangled with gold and a bush of feathers".

As hats became more popular they assumed a variety of shapes and were made in many different materials including silk, velvet, taffeta, leather and felt. Beaver hats, which might cost as much as £4 each, became more readily available and probably cheaper as foreign refugee hatmakers established themselves in England. Squarish flat-topped hats with broad or narrow brims and a style resembling the modern man's bowler were popular amongst middle-class and country-women **(Figs 103 and 107)**. Fashionable ladies preferred more exaggerated high crowned styles **(Figs 105** and **106)** although, probably because of the elaborate hairstyles, they still tended to wear their hats mainly for riding or travelling. All classes invariably wore undercaps or coifs beneath their hats.

Although dark colours were common, hats might be of any colour and those made of thin materials might be quilted or embroidered with coloured silks and gold or silver thread. Hat bands were important and could be of any colour or material, and were often twisted or plaited. Flat, broad bands were embroidered or sewn with jewels, gold and enamelled buttons and studs. Tall single plumes or tufts of feathers were often added, generally at the side or towards the back of the hat. The descriptions of some of the caps and hats received by Queen Elizabeth as New Year gifts show how elaborate these articles might be: 1577–78: "A cap of purple vellat set with eight dozen and six buttons of golde, with a white feather". 1578–79: "A cap of black vellat with thirteen buttons of gold in every one of them either a ruby or diamonde"; and "A hat of tawny taphata embraudered with scorpions of Venice gold". 1599–1600: "One hatte (and a feather) of white tiffany embraudered all over".

Thrummed hats, made of cloth woven with a nap or pile, were common amongst the less fashionable towards the end of the century. A thrummed hat formed part of Falstaff's disguise as a woman in *The Merry Wives of Windsor*.

Large plain hats made of plaited straw were worn by country women when working out of doors in the summer. The art of plaiting straws and sewing the lengths together to form the required shape first originated in Tuscany and was flourishing there in the sixteenth century. It is likely that the English straw-hat industry may have arisen at this time through skilful individuals imitating the earliest Italian straw hats, although the earliest references to straw plaiting and straw hat making in England do not occur until the seventeenth century.

Fig. 103 1587

Fig. 102 1563

Fig. 104 1569

Fig. 105 1573

Fig. 106 1591

Fig. 107 1598

Elizabethan

5 Hoods

French hoods continued to be worn until the end of the century by older or more conservative women, and the hair was worn in rolls on either side of the centre parting. Although the hoods were usually similar in shape to those worn in the 1540's and 1550's there were minor variations and some older women adopted a style which covered the hair completely. The hanging piece at the back tended to become narrower (**Figs 108 and 109**).

During the 1580's a curious article of head-wear made its appearance. It was really a combined hood and cloak which was worn out of doors and was also worn as a sign of mourning, especially by widows. Made of thick material and probably stiffened or padded it was wired to form an arch around and over the head and projecting forward over the face. There was often a slight downward curve in the front, echoing the fashionable heart shape. The hood was attached to the shoulders or occasionally to the waist and the material hung in heavy folds from the back of the head or from the neck. The garment could be full length or waist length as in the example in **Figs 110** and **110A**.

The hood or cap usually associated with Mary Queen of Scots (**Fig. 111**), first began to be worn about the middle of the century, and at first was quite small. It was made of white silk, gauze, or lawn and might be jewelled or edged with lace and trimmed with lace insertion. The cap was worn well back on the head, with the hair showing in waves or curls. The front border was wired to the characteristic heart shape and curved forward over the forehead. By the end of the century this style of hood had become much larger and was a fashion favoured by mature women. Black hoods were worn for mourning.

Fig. 112 shows a bongrace worn with a fashionable hairstyle. The hanging piece at the back of the French hood is turned up and fastened over the top of the head. This fashion also tended to be worn by older women during this period. Young and fashionable women adopted silk or velvet masks to shield their complexions.

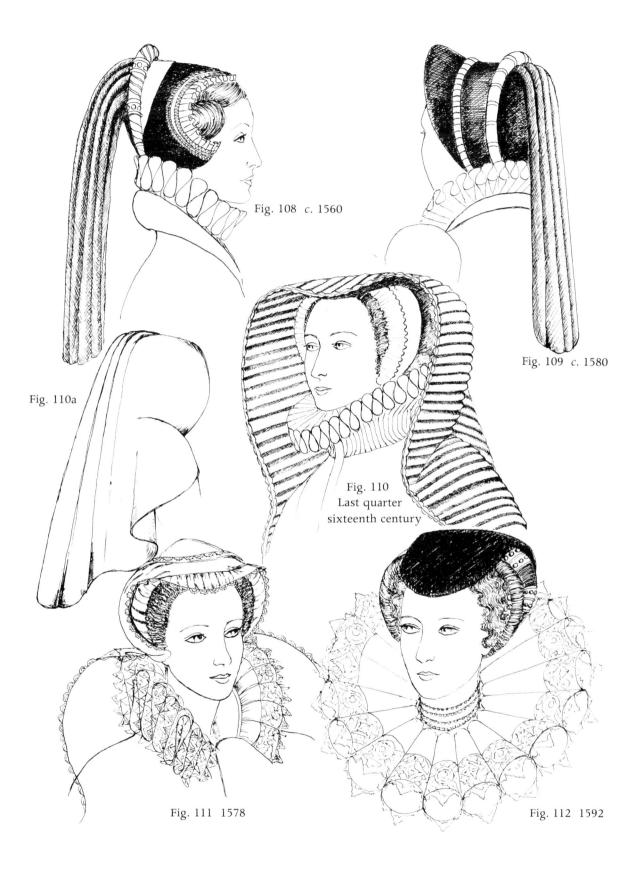

Fig. 108 *c.* 1560

Fig. 109 *c.* 1580

Fig. 110a

Fig. 110
Last quarter
sixteenth century

Fig. 111 1578

Fig. 112 1592

Stuart
1603–1714

The elaborate costume of the late Elizabethan period continued in fashion throughout the reign of James I. The French *wheel* farthingale was favoured by James' wife Anne of Denmark and it remained fashionable until her death in 1619, after which it became much smaller or was discontinued altogether. The skirts were shorter, revealing the feet and ankles. The stiffened bodice continued to be long and narrow until after 1615, when it became less sharply pointed in front. Lavish adornment in the form of jewels, embroidery and lace was still usual. A smaller version of the Elizabethan ruff was still worn, but was frequently unstiffened or *falling* and a new style of lace collar or *band* appeared which was semi-circular in shape and was wired to stand up behind the head. The fan-shaped ruff and high wired collar framing the head were popular until the end of the reign and consequently the high coiffure remained fashionable in order that the head should retain some importance, but by 1619 short hair had become so fashionable that it was the subject of much criticism by the clergy and others, including the King himself.

Towards the end of the reign a change was apparent in the costume of both sexes. The extravagance and artificiality which had been fashionable for more than a century was giving way to the graceful lines and softer colours which characterized the clothing of the reign of Charles I. By about 1630 the farthingale had vanished and skirts were very full, gathered at the waist. The bodice was very high waisted and the neck line was still low, with a *Vandyck* lace edging or a lace collar. A falling ruff with a high-necked bodice was favoured by older women and many middle-class women wore the circular or oval stiffened ruff until the middle of the century. After about 1635 the low décolletage was partially or wholly covered by a deep cape-like collar fastened at the neck, or by a neckerchief, a large square of linen or lawn sometimes edged with lace, which was folded diagonally and draped over the shoulders like a shawl.

There were various styles of sleeves. They were often close fitting, finished with a cuff and sometimes with a long hanging outer sleeve. Later the sleeve became full, ending below the elbow and after about 1640 the whole forearm was revealed. This sleeve was finished by a broad cuff or by the hanging frills or ruffles of the chemise sleeve.

The hairstyles matched the simpler more elegant style of dressing and to be bare-headed was still fashionable for younger women, the elderly preferring some form of head covering. The soft hood became popular among all classes during the 1640's and during the same period white caps or coifs and tall-crowned broad-brimmed hats were commonly worn, especially by middle class and country women who continued to wear them until shortly after the Restoration. The advent of elaborately curled hairstyles in the late 1660's caused the majority of women to wear the more adaptable soft hood in preference to any form of hat except for riding. Pearls were almost the only jewels worn and were generally in the form of earrings and necklaces or threaded in the hair.

Throughout the period of the Commonwealth and Protectorate little change occurred in the style of dress. The main feature as far as women were concerned was that waist lines returned to their natural level. The neckline was rounder and revealed more of the shoulders. After the Restoration these features became more pronounced, with a return to tight lacing to achieve a small waist. The wide low neckline showed an edging of silk frills or lace which was probably attached to the chemise. The full sleeves were gathered in above the elbow and trimmed with ribbons, the chemise sleeves showing below in puffs and ruffles. The skirts were very full and were gathered or pleated at the waist and worn over numerous petticoats. The open-fronted style returned in the 1670's. It was caught back at the sides with ribbon bows revealing a con-trasting underskirt and then fell in folds behind forming a train. This type of gown continued in fashion until the reign of William and Mary, when changes occurred in the structure of the bodice, which was then either stiffened or worn over a corset. The front was open over a stomacher and was either laced across or decorated with a vertical row of ribbon bows or jewelled ornaments. Sleeves were generally close fitting, ending above the elbow with an upturned cuff beneath which fell the long ruffles of silk or lace. A notable feature of late Stuart costume was the extensive use not only of lace but of ribbon loops and bows on bodice, sleeves and skirt. This form of decoration was extended to the headdress, culminating in the *fontange*. Lace was an expensive item and a complete *head* of French point Mechlin or Brussels lace, together with matching ruffles and *tucker* (neck edging) could cost as much as £80.

Towards the end of the period the tall elegant silhouette enhanced by the high headdress began to change as the hoop, a new form of the farthingale, made its appearance after an absence of nearly a century.

Stuart

1 Hairstyles 1603–1660

The high oval-shaped hair arrangement so fashionable during the last 10 or 12 years of the Elizabethan period continued to be high fashion for the first half of James I's reign. The hair was brushed up high over a pad or arched wire frame **(Fig. 113)**. The back hair was drawn back in a flat topped bun set rather high. Very narrow plaits were sometimes arranged in various ways across the back of the head or round the bun, but cauls or nets were also still worn. As an alternative to the bun the hair might be drawn up smoothly from the neck and over the head towards the front so as to increase the fullness and height. Plumes set behind and slightly to the side of the high framework were worn by the fashionable, at Court, and for special occasions. Ribbon bows and jewelled ornaments similar to those of the previous reign decorated the front hair and were also placed at the back. Borders of goldsmith's work and jewels were still worn, but appeared to be less popular than single ornaments. High foreheads were still admired. In Shakespeare's *Merry Wives of Windsor* Falstaff says to Mistress Ford: "Thou hast the right arched beauty of the brow that becomes the ship-tire, tire valiant or any tire of Venetian admittance." The tires referred to were the fashionable high styles of the period, the ship-tire being one adorned with floating ribbons.

From about 1608 the height of these tires began to decrease gradually and by 1614 fashionable women had replaced wire frames by pads or rolls. The hair was at first brushed slightly up, but more usually it was taken straight back from the forehead, crimped or frizzed with a certain amount of fluffiness at the sides and as before fastened into a bun at the back. It was very fashionable to have the side hair cut short about level with the ear lobes and brushed to stand away slightly from the sides of the head. In some cases the front hair was shortened over the top of the head also **(Fig. 114)**. Jewelled hair ornaments were not now so fashionable, but knots of ribbon and short white ostrich plumes or bunches of egret's feathers, like elongated shaving brushes were worn.

From about 1625 there began to be a change in the style of hairdressing. The hair was parted on either side and the centre portion was drawn back and arranged with the rest of the back hair into a high flat bun. The side hair was still short and was frizzed or hung in ringlets and a straight forehead fringe was usual **(Fig. 115)**. Within a few years this fringe had given place to thin curls arranged carefully. Later these were fewer and tended to be only at the temples. The side hair became longer and was either loosely curled or formed into ringlets **(Figs 116 and 118)**. Sometimes a longer ringlet or curl was allowed to hang down over the neck or to lie across one shoulder. The back hair was either brushed up and braided into a bun together with the ends of the front hair or was parted and taken to either side to increase the mass of curls **(Fig. 117)**. The coils of the bun were intertwined or encircled by strings of pearls or ribbons which were tied in knots or bows, and plumes were also worn. Pear-shaped pearls were fashionable and were universally worn as earrings and occasionally as hair ornaments.

Fig. 113 *c.* 1610

Fig. 114 *c.* 1615

Fig. 115 1620–1635

Fig. 116 1640

Fig. 117 1640

Fig. 118 *c.* 1639

Stuart

2 Hoods and veils 1603–1660

The French hood worn either in the ordinary manner or with the back flap turned up as a *bongrace* was a dying fashion in the early Stuart period and found favour only among elderly women or widows, who sometimes wore it over a coif and forehead cloth in the Elizabethan manner described on page 57. Usually, however, the hood tended to be smaller and to be worn at the back of the head sometimes with a slight peak in front.

The hood of *Mary Stuart* style, which had increased considerably in size towards the end of the sixteenth century became a favourite form of headdress for many women during the early years of the seventeenth century. It was nearly always made of white lace or lawn edged and trimmed with lace. The wide border was wired (or starched) so as to stand away from the head on either side and then curve sharply down over the forehead (**Figs 119 and 120**). The back of the hood fitted the head closely and sometimes a hanging flap was attached which could be worn as a *bongrace*. This style of headdress, like the French hood, was gradually adopted by elderly women during the 1620's and within a few years the fashion died out.

Another headdress which was worn during the first half of the century and especially between 1620 and 1630 was a cap or *shadow* made of linen, lawn, lace or other fine material which was unstiffened but was shaped to curve round the front of the head whilst the back fell straight (**Fig. 121**).

The great hood which had appeared during the latter part of Elizabeth's reign and which had been used out of doors and for mourning continued to be worn for the same purposes during the first quarter of the seventeenth century. In shape and size it was similar to the earlier examples, being curved in at neck or waist and having a peak or dip over the forehead. After about 1620 the curve around the head became smaller, although the back drapery was long, reaching to the feet. This hood continued to be worn by elderly women, especially widows, for some 20 years after its use had been generally discontinued in the 1620's.

Large square veils of thin material were sometimes worn at this period, especially by young widows. One corner was turned back or cut away and the edge was stiffened lightly to stand away from the sides of the head. At the back the veil fell freely to the ground (**Fig. 122**). Towards the middle of the century this type of veil was no longer stiffened. The corner was left in position and formed a peak over the forehead (**Fig. 123**).

Although most head coverings might be worn in or out of doors it was fashionable throughout the period to go bareheaded. To protect the complexion in summer short veils of fine material were draped over the head and face (**Fig. 124**). The kerchief was also worn occasionally. This consisted of a square of fabric edged with lace folded diagonally and placed across the head with the point at the back.

Fig. 119 1620

Fig. 120 1614

Fig. 121 1620–1625

Fig. 122 c. 1620

Fig. 123 c. 1650

Fig. 124 1644

Stuart

3 Coifs and hoods
1603–1660

Coifs, like hats, were more usually worn by lower- or middle-class women who did not wish to adopt elaborate hairstyles; or else they were worn for informal everyday wear either alone or under hats. They were, at first, similar to those worn in the sixteenth century, being close fitting, made in one piece and seamed along the top. They were elaborately embroidered and were hemmed along the neck edge to take the running strings which were tied under the chin. These coifs were often worn with a matching forehead cloth in a similar manner to those of the Elizabethan period.

The later style of coif, which was worn chiefly between 1625 and 1660, was usually of white linen edged with lace or cutwork and was shaped to fit over the bun of hair (**Figs 125, 126 and 127**). The former example was cut in one piece joined down the back by seaming of needlepoint lace and with extra material gathered into fullness at the crown, with a drawstring at the neck. The front band was decorated with cutwork with needlepoint fillings and edged with bobbin lace. **Fig. 126** shows a plain coif worn by a working-class woman.

For wear out of doors close-fitting soft hoods to cover the high hairstyles were first adopted quite early in the period, but became more popular from about 1640 onwards. They were made of double material or with a double thickness at the front edge, which was then rolled or folded back in a cuff to form a squarish frame for the face. The ends were tied under the chin and were either formed into a bow or neatly tucked out of sight. Black or dark colours were usual, but white and colours were also worn (**Figs 129 and 130**). In 1664 Pepys mentions his wife going to church on Whit Sunday wearing a new yellow birdseye hood, "as the fashion is now", and in a comedy written in 1685 a yellow hood is described as suitable Sunday finery for a middle-class woman. Hoods were sometimes worn over coifs.

Masks, usually made of black velvet, satin or silk were also worn out of doors, possibly as disguise but also very likely as protection for the complexion against winter winds. They were used throughout the century. Whole masks covering the face were known as *vizards* and were kept in place by a round bead attached to the inside and held between the teeth. Half masks were fastened by strings round the back of the head. **Fig. 128** shows the type of hood and veil adopted by older widows during this period. There were a number of variations but all had the *widow's peak* over the forehead.

Fig. 125 1625–1650

Fig. 126 Mid seventeenth century

Fig. 127 1640

Fig. 128 c. 1650

Fig. 129 First quarter seventeenth century

Fig. 130 1643

Stuart

4 Hats

Hats in similar styles to those of the later years of Elizabeth's reign continued to be worn for the first few years of the Stuart era. The high, heavily decorated hairstyles precluded the wearing of hats and fashionable women wore them solely for riding or travelling.

The high crowned type with a round top was popular among both the upper and middle classes. The brim was of medium width and might occasionally be turned up at one side. Decorations consisted of plumes and bands of plaited or twisted material or broad swathes of gauze and silk. Jewels were sometimes added **(Fig. 131)**.

As in the previous period, the wearing of hats was common amongst middle-class and country-women, who always wore them over linen coifs with their hair rather raised at the forehead. Young married women sometimes went bare-headed like their unmarried sisters, but more usually they wore the coif and hat.

After 1625 a broader brimmed style of hat with a lower crown trimmed with a hatband and sometimes with sweeping ostrich plumes was worn by fashionable ladies for riding **(Fig. 132)**. This hat, the brim of which could be either flat and level, wavy, or turned up at the side, is usually thought of as the *cavalier* style but it was also adopted by the middle classes, who wore either a high or low crowned version with a flat top known as a *sugar loaf* and with a plain or plaited band **(Figs 134 and 135)**. Hats of this type, now invariably made of felt or beaver, continued to be worn until the Restoration, when hoods became generally popular with all classes. Even then, of course, hats were still thought suitable for riding. John Evelyn in 1666 saw the Queen "in her cavalier riding habite, hat and feather, and horseman's coate".

The crownless linen coif with separate front-let illustrated in **Fig. 133** was probably made to wear beneath a hat, but coifs or caps worn with hats were becoming less usual even among the middle classes, and portraits of the period show that some women preferred to wear their hair plainly dressed beneath their hats **(Fig. 134)**.

Some of the headwear of the early Stuart period already described may be recognized in the report of the Venetian ambassador to his government in 1618. He considered the costume of Englishwomen worthy of detailed description. "... They are so variously adjusted and dress so well", and he describes their headwear, including the lace caps which the Venetian women called *mushrooms*. "... Others wear hats of various shapes: others wear a very small top knot. Some wear a moderate sized silk kerchief surmounted by a bit of crape. ... Others have black velvet hoods or wear embroidered caps covering the whole head whilst others wear their hair uncovered and curled all over, up to the very plait of the tresses ... wearing moreover the plume on the head, sometimes upright sometimes at the back and sometimes even transverse. ...."

Fig. 131 *c.* 1614

Fig. 132 *c.* 1630

Fig. 133 Mid seventeenth century

Fig. 134 1644

Fig. 135 1645

Stuart

5 Hairstyles 1660-1714

Throughout the middle years of the seventeenth century the style of women's hair remained unaltered. The hair was still drawn back from the forehead and coiled into a flat bun high at the back of the head, whilst the side ringlets were almost shoulder length. Forehead curls were not usual, but small ones reappeared with the more elaborate coiffures in the 1660's. For a decade or so after the Restoration the long side hair was wired to stand away from the head and then hung vertically in masses of ringlets or corkscrew curls. The front hair was still brushed straight back with a coiled or plaited bun at the back of the head (**Fig. 136**).

Hair dye and the use of false hair became fashionable once again. In 1665, 1666 and 1667 Samuel Pepys made references in his Diary to his wife wearing fair hair or "white locks" which he disliked because it was not natural although he thought she looked very pretty. In one instance he mentions helping her to buy a "fair pair of locks". Pepys also refers to the Queen's ladies at Whitehall wearing masculine riding habits with periwigs and hats. Another writer in 1663 commented on women striving to be like men when they rode on horseback or in coaches, wearing plush caps full of ribbons and feathers and long periwigs similar to those worn by men. It seems probable, however, that this fashion was confined mainly to ladies of the court.

From about 1670 the wiring out of the side hair ceased and curls were once more allowed to touch the cheeks with one or two long ringlets lying over the shoulders and the occasional wispy curl on the forehead. Between 1670 and 1680 several other styles were introduced and became popular. The first of these, known as the *Hurluberlu*, was created in Paris in 1671 and consisted of a mass of close set roll curls all over the head. The back hair was formed into a bun with long ringlets which strayed over the shoulders and nape of the neck. Another style, sometimes called the *Taure* or *bullhead*, had a mass of curls over the forehead.

From about 1680 centre partings became usual with masses of curls on either side (**Fig. 137**). In all these styles the back hair was arranged in the same way, with a bun and stray ringlets which in many cases may well have been artificial. After 1690 the curls and waves were gradually dressed higher towards the front of the head (**Fig. 140**) and often appeared as two peaks on either side of the parting. Sometimes the front hair was arranged over pads or over a wire known as a *Palisade*, and artificial curls might be added. This built-up coiffure was known as the *Tour* and was often decorated with ribbon bows called *Knots*. The top-knot was a large bow worn on top of the head. Jewel-headed pins or *firmaments* were also worn (**Fig. 141**). All the curls in this coiffure had their own name and place—*cruches* were small curls on the forehead a *passagère* was a lock near the temple, whilst *confidants* hung about the ears. *Crêve-cœurs* or *heart-breakers* were the ringlets at the nape of the neck.

The curls were formed with curling irons or with curl papers fastened with lead and setting lotions containing gum arabic were used. Many recipes were available for dealing with almost every hair condition and for dyeing the hair black, a colour which was much in vogue during the last quarter of the century. In the *Ladies Dictionary* printed in 1694 it was stated that "a mixture of bark of oak root, green husks of walnuts, the deepest and oldest red wine and oil of myrtle will turn any coloured hair as black as jet".

The high hairstyles whether worn alone or with the *fontange* (see next page) reached the peak of popularity during the 1690's but by the early years of Queen Anne's reign were going rapidly out of fashion. The cap shown in **Fig. 139** is described on the following page.

Fig. 136   *c.* 1660

Fig. 137   1680

Fig. 138   1670–1680

Fig. 139   *c.* 1685

Fig. 140   *c.* 1690

Fig. 141   *c.* 1690

Stuart

6 Headdress 1685–1714

The most remarkable headdress of the Stuart period was named after Mlle. Fontanges, a mistress of Louis XIV, who was supposed to have started the fashion in 1679. The story goes that while she was out riding her hair became disarranged and she tied it up with ribbon. It seems more likely, however, that this episode may have been the origin of the top-knot and that the elaborate headdress which bears the young woman's name was a development of the cornet, a kind of cap or coif with long side pieces which either hung down on each side of the face or floated behind to waist level. This cap was usually made of lace, lawn, or gauze and might have an upstanding frill or puffed up fold of material in front (**Fig. 142**; see also **Fig. 139** on previous page). Whatever its origin the fontange made its first appearance in England towards 1690, reaching its maximum height at the turn of the century, and seems to have completely vanished from the scene by the end of Queen Anne's reign.

The close fitting cap worn at the back of the head had two long pieces or *lappets* hanging down behind (sometimes these were pinned to the crown), and in front were two or three upstanding tiers of lawn or lace arranged in pleats, flutes or puffs (**Figs 143 and 145**). Sometimes these tiers grew narrower towards the top, sometimes they were shaped like a half-closed fan widening out at the top. They were either starched or supported by a wire frame called a *commode* and sometimes had a pronounced forward tilt. At other times the arrangement was more or less upright. Many examples of this headdress were decorated with knots of ribbon and the front hair was often raised in a *tour* as already described (**Fig. 144**).

For outdoor wear black or coloured silk hoods were usual. These were larger and more loose fitting than those which had been worn during the middle years of the seventeenth century. They were draped over the cap of the fontange and tied loosely in front over the bosom.

Straw hats were common amongst country women who wore them over coifs or hoods (**Fig. 146**). The brims were of varying widths and could be pulled down on either side with ribbons which were tied under the chin. According to some authorities these country straw hats were sometimes worn by Court ladies in the reign of Queen Anne, but it was not until towards the middle of the eighteenth century that hats became generally popular amongst all classes.

Fig. 142 1689

Fig. 143 c. 1690

Fig. 144 1688

Fig. 145 c. 1694

Fig. 146 1697

Georgian Part 1
1714–1790

The eighteenth century is notable for two tendencies in the costume of both sexes, which vied with one another throughout the greater part of the period. The one was a mode of elaboration and formality, the other a taste for simplicity. The desire for a more comfortable style of clothing may have been inspired by the English love of country life and outdoor activities, a characteristic which became strongly developed during this period; or the contrast between the two styles of dress may have symbolized the struggle between traditional class distinction on the one hand and the effects of inevitable social change on the other. Whatever the reasons it was apparent that for the first time in history fashion was no longer the prerogative of the upper classes. Many features of working-class clothing were adopted by men in all walks of life, and except for Court wear and the most formal occasions this plainer style of dressing became universal. From 1760 to 1780 there was a period of exaggerated fashion and an ostentatious display of luxury which was largely the result of successful commercial activity by many in India and the West Indies. A distinction was beginning to be made between *dress* or best wear and *undress* or informal everyday wear, but this was not so apparent in women's clothing.

Feminine dress on the whole retained an elegant simplicity throughout the period and changes were chiefly confined to the modification of existing styles or alteration in details. The most noticeable feature of the silhouette was the hooped skirt, of which there were several versions. The first style to become fashionable was the bell or dome shape which was worn from about 1710 to 1780. The fan shape appeared towards the end of Queen Anne's reign but did not become popular until 1740. This type was flattened at the front and back so that the hem dipped to the floor and rose up at either side. The third style of hoop, which also became fashionable about 1740 was elongated, that is, extremely wide at the sides but flat at front and back. Hoops reached their widest dimensions in the 1750's and were popular with all classes, although many working-class women wore smaller hoops or quilted petticoats instead. A unique feature of the eighteenth century was the gown with the *sack* back which first appeared about 1720, and in a number of variations this style remained fashionable for many years. Although the material of the working-class women's clothing was plainer than the superb silks and satins frequently used for the dress of wealthier women the gowns themselves were in the fashionable styles of the time. In 1782 a foreign traveller noted that Englishwomen generally were so interested in clothes that even the poorest servant was careful to be in the fashion, particularly in hats and bonnets.

The low, simply dressed hairstyle which followed the sudden disappearance of the fontange at the end of Queen Anne's reign remained unchanged for many years in spite of the obvious disparity between the small heads, with their little caps, and the great hooped skirts. It is probable that only a minority wore the exaggerated hairstyles and great wigs which were fashionable in the 1770's, although most women appeared to follow the trend for higher styles by raising their hair over pads or rolls and by "frizzing" or back combing. A French visitor to England observed that English ladies were so conscious of their beauty that they tended to neglect their dress and "the care of dressing, that of dressing the hair above all, is observable in only a small number of ladies who . . . have resolution enough to go through all the operations of the hairdresser. The country life led by these ladies during the greater part of the year and the freedom which accompanies that way of life make them continue an agreeable negligence in dress which never gives disgust."

Englishwomen of the late eighteenth century undoubtedly regarded their hats as the most important part of their costume and they knew how to wear them with the right air of elegance and grace.

In this century the straw plait industry expanded greatly owing to the production in Italy of a fine wheat straw which was used eventually in making the famous Leghorn plait which, because of its quality, was much sought after in England and other countries where straw hats were made. In addition to ready-made hats, straw and chip plait was imported and made up into hats and bonnets by milliners, cap makers and mantua makers. *Chip*, which was made from strips of willow or poplar plaited in the same way as straw was mentioned frequently throughout the eighteenth and early nineteenth centuries and was used considerably as an alternative to straw. Such was the growth of the trade that separate establishments were set up to deal with the making of straw hats and, in course of time, with all types of hats worn by women. In the eighteenth century milliners dealt with the great variety of trimmings and ornaments so popular at the period and were not specifically concerned with the making of hats. It was not until well into the nineteenth century that milliners became associated with hat making and trimming exclusively.

Georgian

1 Hairstyles 1714–1770

After the disappearance of the tour and the fontange in the reign of Queen Anne the hair-dressing styles became relatively simple. Although forehead curls and *favourites* were worn by many for the first few years of George I's reign the emphasis was tending to be towards the back of the head, where the hair was coiled into a small bun and one or two long locks hung behind or lay over the shoulders. After going out of fashion generally this style was still worn at Court.

After about 1720 the majority of women of all classes preferred to wear a simple style, with the hair drawn loosely back from the forehead with a bun on top and slightly towards the back of the head. Sometimes curls were arranged round the face or stray locks allowed to fall casually about the temples (**Figs 147** and **148**).

This method of dressing the hair remained generally fashionable until after the middle of the century. A style which became popular in the 1730's, especially for formal occasions was the "Dutch" coiffure (**Fig. 149**). The hair was drawn back from the face in loose waves, sometimes with a centre parting, and fell in ringlets or wavy locks at the back of the neck. On dress occasions no cap was worn with this style, but pearls were entwined in the hair or knots of ribbon were used as decoration.

Another style worn during the same period was a false "head" of close curls called a *tête de mouton*. This, together with the "Dutch" style remained fashionable for about 20 years. Top-knots, bunches of ribbon loops in various colours, artificial flowers, jewels and pearls set on ribbons or pins were worn as decorations. A *pom-pom* set in front or slightly to the side of the head was one of the most popular hair ornaments throughout the middle years of the century. Ribbons, small feathers such as ostrich plume tips, lace flowers, butterflies and jewels in any combination went to make up this decoration (**Figs 150, 151** and **152**). Wigs were worn but usually only for riding or perhaps at Court.

White, grey or coloured hair powder seems to have been used by many women throughout the early part of this period, but apparently only for special occasions although its use became more and more general with the increasing elaboration of the coiffures in the 1760's. About the middle of the decade rolls of horsehair, tow or wool began to be used to raise up the front hair, which was often frizzed or arranged in roll curls set horizontally round the head (**Fig. 152**), False hair and pomatum began to be used also in order to give additional height and body to the coiffure. The back hair was still turned up and arranged in a knot on top or at the back of the head. By 1770 the fashionable hair style for dress wear was quite high and large plumes were being worn.

The pomatum or paste which was used to stiffen up the hair and hold the powder was made of various substances such as hog's grease, tallow, or a mixture of beef marrow and oil.

Fig. 148 c. 1730

Fig. 147 1720

Fig. 149 1735

Fig. 150 1761

Fig. 151 1760–1765

Fig. 152 1760–1770

Georgian

2 Hairstyles 1770–1780

In the 1770's the fashionable hairstyle reached extraordinary heights and was decorated with a fantastic number and variety of ornaments. The hair was dressed over pads or cushions stuffed with wool or horsehair and all styles and shapes were built over these cushion foundations. Smaller pads and wire supports were also used. Various arrangements were popular, but an oval or egg shape, and a heart or crescent shape were the most usual. Large roll curls were placed more or less horizontally on each side of the head sometimes reaching the top, as in **Fig. 154A**, sometimes in small groups behind or around the ears. At least one curl generally hung vertically or horizontally behind and below the ear. The back hair was usually dressed in a *chignon*, a wide swathe of hair hanging down behind and then looped up and fastened with long pins or bound in the middle with ribbon **(Fig. 155)**. The general appearance of the chignon was flat and smooth. Later the back hair might be plaited, or twisted **(Figs 154B and 157)**. In the *Lady's Magazine* for May 1775 the fashionable style for full dress was described as being "all over in small curls and pearl pins, starred leaves and large white or coloured feathers, two drop curls at the ears and powder universal". The same magazine described the headdress illustrated in **Fig. 156** as being "ushered in at the beginning of Spring with a small tuft of feathers which was soon changed to two or three distinct ones of the largest size, some pink or blue but most generally white and placed remarkably flat, with a rose of ribbons on the forepart and a knot suspended at the back of the head—with two, three or four large curls down the sides with bottom curl nearly upright. The bag (chignon) not so low as the chin, small and smooth at the bottom."

In 1779 the *London Magazine* reported "the ladies dress their hair very high. They have just introduced a method of plaiting the hair behind in one row up the middle of the head on which they place large bows of ribbon" **(Fig. 157)**. In 1778 Lady Clermont wrote to the Duchess of Devonshire from Fontainebleau: "The heads are full as high as last year, but not near so high as in England."

The art of preparing these elaborate "heads" involved the expenditure of much time and skill and good hairdressers or *friseurs* were much in demand. One of these, James Stewart, who wrote a treatise on the subject, warned those ladies who wished to dress their own hair that they would find it very troublesome and tedious. "Those who are willing to surmount these difficulties, and can spare two or three hours with patience and perseverance, may in time, by practice make some progress and proficiency."

It is not surprising that after spending several hours having the hair cut, pomaded, curled, frizzed, powdered and finally loaded with ornaments or feathers and draped with gauze or ribbons women allowed these structures to remain untouched for several weeks or even months. Stewart's instructions were explicit: "At night all that is required is to take off cap and ornaments and nothing need to touched but the curls, do them in nice long rollers firmly. The hair should never be combed at night as this may cause violent head-aches next day. A large net fillet with strings drawn tight round face and neck, this with a fine lawn handerchief is sufficient night covering for the head." Next day the curls were to be unpinned and the surface of the hair "raked hard" to remove loose powder, then pomading, frizzing and powdering as before. "In this manner you may proceed every day for two or three months, or as long as the lady chooses, till the hair gets straight and clotted and matted with dirty powder. Then it is absolutely necessary to comb it out." Detailed instructions were given for this procedure. In view of the unpleasant consequences of having heads dressed "to keep" many women, even those in unfashionable circles, preferred to wear whole wigs. In either case a head scratcher was a useful article to have at hand. This might be made of ivory, silver or gold and sometimes the handle was set with jewels **(Fig. 158)**. Wigs were curled by means of heated clay rollers. The strands of hair were wound round these and pressed with special circular-ended tongs.

Fig. 153 1773

Fig. 154a *c.* 1775

Fig. 154b *c.* 1775

Fig. 155 1776

Fig. 156 1775

Fig. 158

Fig. 157 1779

Georgian

3 Hairstyles 1780–1790

By 1780 heads had reached the extremity of height and elaboration. As well as enormous plumes of every colour, ornaments of every description were added to the mass of powdered, curled and frizzled hair. These included bunches of flowers, fruit, vegetables, ribbons, lace, jewelled pins, ornaments of blown glass and in extreme cases such things as models of complete gardens, baskets of flowers or plates of fruit. In 1782 Fanny Burney described Lady Say and Sele's head as being "full of feathers, flowers, jewels and gew-gaws, and as high as Lady Archer's". However, by the middle of the 1780's lofty headdresses were no longer fashionable, although many women were loth to change and the hairdressing processes especially for Court wear were still as prolonged as ever. In August 1786 Fanny Burney tells of being up at 6 a.m. to have her hair done for a State occasion. After two hours it was still not finished and receiving a summons to attend the Queen she ran down without a cap. She says she felt very foolish with her uncovered head. Evidently it was considered improper to appear before the Royal Family without a cap, although it was not customary for the Royal ladies themselves to wear caps.

In this decade the *toupée*, as the front portion of the hair arrangement was called, was fuller than it had been and tended to width rather than height, the hair being frizzed to stand away from the head. The ears were now covered instead of being partially or completely exposed, as they had been in the 1770's (**Figs 159** and **160**). A style called the *hérisson* or *hedgehog* was extremely popular in England and France from 1777. This was an example of extreme frizzling carried out on the half-moon shaped toupee. Hair powder of various colours was available, including red and yellow, but white was considered the most flattering, although careful consideration was given to the effect of various colours on the complexion.

In 1787, at the celebrations in honour of the King's birthday, the ladies were described as having heads dressed very wide in curls and wearing caps with flowers and plumes. It seems that the wearing of feathers at Court persisted in spite of the Queen's disapproval. On one occasion the Duchess of Devonshire appeared with feathers on a headdress that for magnitude and height surpassed anything that had previously been seen. The Queen, who had forbidden such exaggerated styles, appeared without feathers, her hair simply arranged and decorated with diamonds and pearls.

In general throughout the 1780's the hair was either crimped or frizzed all over the head with large curls resting on the neck or flowing behind. As an alternative the hair at the back could still be arranged in the various types of chignon or in a *club* or *catogan* similar to that worn by men. The long tail of hair was brushed smooth and flat, then turned up and over into a large loop which was then fastened round the middle with a ribbon giving the appearance of a vertical bow. This style was most often adopted for riding.

It became increasingly fashionable in the course of the 1780's for the hair to be dressed with studied carelessness in loose curls or waves all over the head and hanging in ringlets or long tresses down the back, sometimes to the waist (**Figs 161** and **162**). Elaborate trimmings were gradually discarded, although fancy caps, pearls and ribbon continued to be popular, but many women preferred to wear no ornaments at all.

Fig. 159 1782

Fig. 160 1782

Fig. 161 1785

Fig. 162 1784

Georgian

4 Caps 1714–1770

Many kinds of caps were worn by women of all classes throughout the eighteenth century from the time the fontange went out of fashion in the reign of Queen Anne, but they were most universally worn during the reigns of the first two Georges.

There were several main types, each of which had a number of variations. The "heads", as they were called during this period were always of white fabric or lace and were worn both indoors and out and were very frequently worn under hats. Plain untrimmed caps were worn by working-class women and by other women for day wear. Dress caps were often trimmed with or made entirely of lace.

Very early in the century the small round cap with lappets, which had formed the foundation for the fontange, was worn with the fan-like frill, now much smaller, arranged in a horizontal position over the front of the head instead of being wired up vertically. About 1720 this style of cap, now called a *pinner*, was superseded by the version shown in **Fig. 165**, which was worn flat on top of the head and was bordered with a single or double frill and trimmed with coloured ribbon. When the lappets or streamers were present they hung down behind, or could be pinned up to the crown of the cap according to choice. A little bunch of artificial flowers or ribbon or a jewelled ornament might be set at the front or side for special occasions.

Another type of small cap made its appearance about 1730. Like the pinner it had a frilled border but this extended round the front only and frequently had a V-shaped pleat in the centre. The back was plain and could completely cover the back of the head or be quite shallow, revealing much of the back hair. Like the pinner, this round cap could be worn with or without lappets. When present these streamers formed an extension of the frilled border and could be pinned up. Sometimes lappets were double, but these were usually allowed to hang freely. Trimmings of ribbon, flowers or jewels were present

on caps intended for grand occasions. Towards the middle of the century the frill became wider on either side of the head and was starched or wired to stand out. **Fig. 163**, **Fig. 164** and **Fig. 166** show versions of this cap. Those with side lappets were by mid-century more often worn by older women, who tied them under the chin with a ribbon bow. Flowers or ribbons were sometimes placed in the centre front of the cap (**Fig. 166**). Another version of this winged style appeared about 1760 and also seems to have been preferred by older women. In this form the wings were wired into semi-circles high on the head and were tilted slightly forward. A pom-pon ornament was often placed in the hair or on the dip of the cap itself. The short lappets were pinned up or sometimes left off altogether. Occasionally a scarf or kerchief was draped over the cap and tied under the chin. The *mob* cap had a full crown surrounded by a fairly broad ribbon often tied in a bow or arranged in several loops at the front. The frilled front edge of the cap deepened into lappets at the sides. These could be quite long, but were usually just below shoulder length and were either allowed to hang loose or were pinned or tied under the chin. **Figs 167** and **168** show plain mobs worn by working-class women. These caps were worn throughout the century, becoming especially popular during the reign of George II, and were always for informal or undress wear. Various other small caps appeared during the 1750's including the *Joan* or *Quaker* cap, a bonnet style tied under the chin.

By 1760 many caps had become very small or had gone out of fashion, including the form of mob already described although it continued to be worn by older working-class women until the end of the century. The *Ranelagh mob*, worn informally during the 1760's was simply a square of fine material folded diagonally and placed over the head with the ends fastened under the chin or crossed over the throat and tied at the back. This fashion was said to have been copied from the market women who tied up their heads in this manner. Throughout this century the caps, although usually named according to their shapes, might also be called after the type of lace or the trimmings on them, for example the *Mechlenburgh* cap or *Brussels* head.

Fig. 163 c. 1740

Fig. 165 c. 1730

Fig. 164 c. 1730

Fig. 166 1740–1750

Fig. 167 1733

Fig. 169 c. 1762

Fig. 168 1760

Georgian

5 Caps 1770–1790

As the hairdressing became higher and more elaborate the undress caps, that is, those worn informally, grew extremely large in order to accommodate the coiffure, whilst those intended for "dress" became comparatively small and were generally set on top of the pile of hair.

Although the mob cap varied in size according to the hairstyles it was rather out of fashion during the 1770's, when the hair was at its highest, but it became popular again during the 1780's when it was extremely large (**Fig. 174**). Of necessity it was generally made of lightweight material such as lawn or muslin and trimmed with lace. The falling frills could be either single or double; the ribbon bands and bows were correspondingly large. Smaller mob caps became fashionable after about 1790. A cap known as the French nightcap or *dormeuse* was worn during this period and was particularly fashionable when it was at its largest during the 1770's. Like the mob it had a loose easy-fitting crown which was trimmed or swathed with broad ribbon finished with a bow. On either side of the cap curving round the cheeks were frills, single or double, often pleated or gathered and usually either made of lace or lace-trimmed (**Fig. 170**). A "gable" shaped version of this cap was also worn, especially as the hair styles grew higher. In this style the side frills were frequently retained, but sometimes other trimmings or edging were used. The cap was always fastened under the chin and ribbon bows or ruffles of lace decorated the top (**Fig. 172**). Later on the former version of this cap became very small and was perched on top of the hair. Turban style caps were also fashionable from the 1760's and throughout this period. They usually consisted of a scarf or length of lightweight material draped or twisted round the head in various ways, sometimes with hanging ends. Jewels and feathers were often added (**Fig. 171**). "Dress" caps were frequently no more than a puff or twist of gauze or tulle often with long ends floating behind. Flowers, feathers and other ornaments were usually part of this headdress especially for Court wear (**Fig. 173**).

Fig. 170 *c.* 1775

Fig. 171 *c.* 1770

Fig. 172 *c.* 1770

Fig. 173 1789

Fig. 174 Late 1780's

Georgian

6 Hats 1714–1780

Hats made from straw had been worn by country women since the sixteenth century, but it was during the second quarter of the eighteenth that this humble form of headwear became popular and was worn by women of all classes.

The most usual type of straw hat was the *bergère*, a wide-brimmed shallow crowned variety which had been worn by country women for many years (see previous period). The brims were often held down on either side by ribbons attached to the crown and tied under the chin or at the back of the head (**Fig. 175**). These hats became especially fashionable between 1750 and 1760 when the brims were often turned up at the front and back (**Fig. 177**). In this style they were often secured by ribbons or scarves attached beneath the brim and tied under the back hair. This fashion for turned up brims became less usual after 1760 and hats were worn straight for a while (**Fig. 178**) until the rising hairstyles towards the end of the decade made it necessary for them to be tilted forward. It was usual for hats to be worn over the day caps which were so universally fashionable at this period. The exceptions to this custom were riding hats which were of the three-cornered style and were usually worn with a wig (**Fig. 176**). These hats varied considerably in size, becoming smaller during the course of the century. They were made of felt or beaver and were trimmed with a button and loop on the left side or sometimes with a feather fringe along the edge of the brim. Black jockey caps were also worn for riding, but these were often made of less practical materials such as velvet or satin. These too were worn with small wigs or had artificial curls attached.

The hats worn over the elaborately dressed hair of the 1770's were various and necessarily large, although at first quite small hats were fashionable. Many women discarded hats altogether for a time, preferring to wear day caps instead or very high hats which fitted over the entire coiffure (**Fig. 180**). The bergère and other styles were worn at an extreme angle, tilted up behind and down over the forehead (**Fig. 179**). The term *bonnet* now came into use to describe various types of hats, some of which could be likened to the true bonnet style which appeared later in the century. Hats were named after contemporary events, personalities and places. In May 1775 the *Lady's Magazine* described all kinds of hats, among them the *St. James*, made of fine plain chip with blond (lace) bands and white feathers; the *Ranelagh*, made of silk trimmed with chenille and blond, and the *Macaroni*, made of chip with coloured gauze puckered all over. Chip was a favourite material for hats either on its own or covered with silk, satin or lace.

By the end of the 1770's hats had become very large, with heavily trimmed crowns and brims turned up at the back, often with wide ribbons hanging down behind.

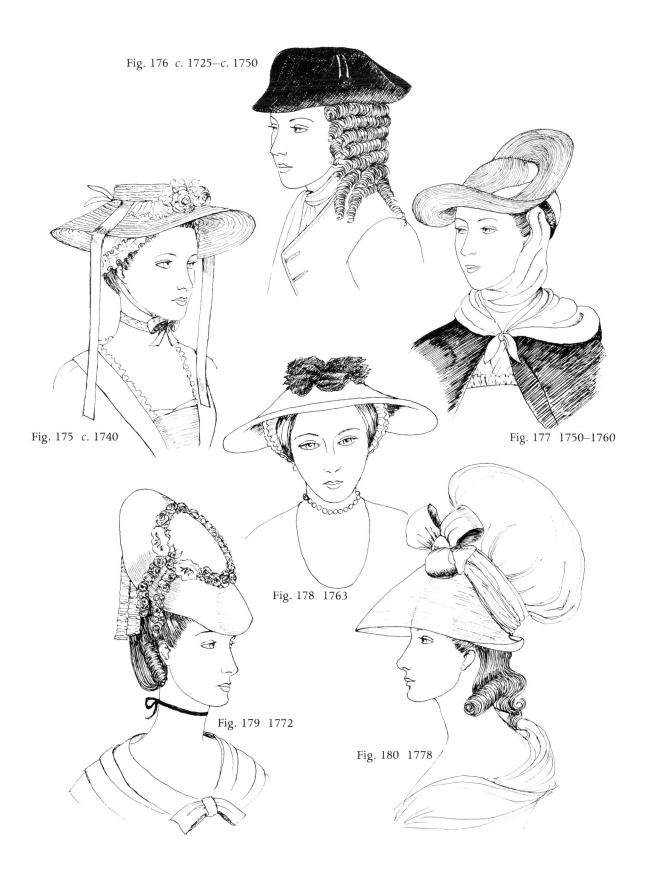

Fig. 176 *c.* 1725–*c.* 1750

Fig. 175 *c.* 1740

Fig. 177 1750–1760

Fig. 178 1763

Fig. 179 1772

Fig. 180 1778

Georgian

7 Hats 1780–1790

In the 1780's all hats were extremely large and from about 1783 were worn either straight on the head or at a variety of angles. The illustrations show examples of one of the two main types of fashionable hats of this decade. All these had stiff crowns and were made of appropriate materials such as straw or felt which might be covered with other fabrics. **Fig. 181** and **Fig. 182** were variations on the bergère or country straw. **Fig. 182** had a shallow crown and stiff brim trimmed with a lace edge or curtain. **Fig. 181** shows a similar style with a more flexible brim which might be broader at the back. Lavish trimmings often included several large feathers.

Another wide brimmed hat with a deep crown was very popular during the middle years of the decade (**Fig. 183**). It was a hat of this style which was worn by the Duchess of Devonshire in the famous portrait by Gainsborough and which subsequently became known as the *picture* hat. These hats were worn at an extreme sideways angle or occasionally tilted backwards. Tall crowned hats of various kinds became fashionable during the late 1780's. **Fig. 184** shows a style sometimes known as a *Theodore* bonnet, which had a cylindrical crown and a sloping brim either narrow or wide. Large veils were frequently worn with these hats, or curtains of lace which were attached all round the edge of the brim. Another popular high hat had a crown which tapered towards the top and the brim was straight or slightly curved (**Fig. 185**). Trimmings consisted chiefly of large plumes and ribbon arranged in every imaginable way, gathered in rosettes, tied in bows or loops, wired or floating freely. Artificial flowers were occasionally used.

Fig. 182 1784

Fig. 181 1785

Fig. 183 1783

Fig. 184 1787

Fig. 185 *c.* 1790

Georgian

8 Hats 1780–1790

The other fashionable type of hat worn during this decade was made of soft material such as silk or gauze with a large puffed up crown and a wide brim. The first examples of these hats were inspired by the exploits of Lunardi, who made the first ascent in a hot-air balloon in 1783. These hats were called *Lunardi* or *balloon* hats, and although these names were discontinued after a year or two the hats themselves continued to be fashionable in one form or another until about 1790. A stiff lining was necessary to support the crowns of these hats and the brims were of chip or were wired round the edges (**Figs 186, 187** and **188**).

Riding hats were worn, not only with riding dress, but with other forms of dress for day wear. The *cocked* form was a favourite from the late 1770's. The brim was turned up or "cocked" on either one or both sides and was held in place by a ribbon rosette or cockade or with a loop attached to the crown and encircling a button on the brim. These hats were often very large and might be made of black or white beaver in winter or of chip or straw in summer (**Fig. 190**). Another style of riding hat had a fairly high crown and a wide flat brim which sometimes curved down at the back. It was trimmed with ribbon or had a hat band with a buckle (**Fig. 189**). Both types of hat were very often decorated with feathers.

The wearing of caps beneath hats was unusual during this period, although mob caps were occasionally seen. The term "dress" and "half dress", applied to hats at this time, meant that they were worn without caps.

Fig. 186 1787

Fig. 187 1788

Fig. 188 1787

Fig. 189 1790

Fig. 190 1786

Georgian

9 Hoods 1714–1790

Hoods of various kinds were worn as head covering out of doors, and sometimes indoors also, and they remained fashionable until the 1760's when they came to be used chiefly by the lower classes and country women.

Many hoods were similar to those worn in the previous period, being soft and sufficiently large to cover both hair and cap. They were either worn alone (**Fig. 191**) or were attached to a shoulder cape or a waist-length cloak or jacket.

All hoods were made on a similar pattern, being gathered or pleated at the back and were made of various materials ranging from velvet and elaborately embroidered or quilted satin to muslin and gauze. Silk hoods were sometimes trimmed with lace, ruching or frills. **Fig. 194** illustrates an original specimen made of cream-coloured quilted satin. The hood is attached to a sack-back jacket.

A popular type of hood during the earlier part of the century was that, shown in **Fig. 192**, which had long pieces down either side of the face. These could either be left hanging or were loosely tied or crossed over under the chin and taken round the neck to be tied again at the back. Hoods were usually worn over caps and the "head" with long lappets and pleated ruffle, shown in the illustration, was often adopted by widows about this time.

Black was popular for hoods but white and other colours were also worn especially for "dress" occasions. Brightly coloured linings were often used in black hoods. **Fig. 195** illustrates an original example which is lined with rose coloured silk. The shoulder cape shown in **Fig. 196** was another variation in the fashion for caped hoods. A so-called *riding-hood* which was also worn for other occasions had a deeper cape and became very fashionable and popular with all classes.

Another type of hood, usually attached to a cape, was made of silk drawn over half hoops of cane thus giving protection from the weather without disarranging the coiffure. This hood appeared in the middle of the century when the hair styles were beginning to rise and was the forerunner of the *calash* (**Fig. 193**). This huge contraption which was not attached to a cape was designed to accommodate the vast headdresses of the 1770's and 1780's. In spite of their size these coverings were very light in weight. Made of thin silk, taffeta or cotton and lined with silk the calash could be folded back when not required and some models had cords for raising the hood when needed. Some form of water proofing was evidently attempted at this period as several existing examples of these hoods are made from a kind of oiled silk or glazed cotton.

Very large hoods, without supporting canes, made of very light thin silk either lined or unlined and edged with lace were also worn over the high "heads". These were usually attached to shoulder capes.

Fig. 191 *c.* 1720

Fig. 192 *c.* 1730

Fig. 193
Last quarter
eighteenth century

Fig. 194
Mid eighteenth century

Fig. 195 1760–1770

Fig. 196 *c.* 1730

Georgian Part 2
1790–1837

Until the French Revolution the history of fashion had been one of gradual evolution, the changes of style and silhouette merging almost imperceptibly from one into another, but the events of 1789 to 1794, affecting as they did all levels of society, also brought about drastic changes in the dress of both sexes. The trend in women's costume towards simplicity of line and the use of cheaper materials, as well as the development of more practical clothes for men, which had been apparent in England for many years became rapidly accelerated during the years of the Revolution. The eighteenth-century interest in classical antiquity was also among the influences which transformed women's fashions at this time. Dresses based on the style of costume worn by the Greeks were already being illustrated in the pages of the fashion journals in 1789–90, and exaggerated versions of these were worn by some Parisian women during the early days of the Revolution. The style which was adopted by the majority of women and worn until about 1810 was extremely simple. Skirts were gathered slightly into very high waistlines and flowed loosely to the feet without shaping. Necklines could be either high or very low and sleeves were long and close fitting or short and often puffed. Tight lacing was discarded entirely and very few underclothes were worn at all, although the flimsy dresses were worn all the year round. Delicate semi-transparent muslin, lawn and cambric in white or pale, cool colours with small patterns replaced the heavy satins and rich brocades of former times. Shawls, cloaks and long wide scarves were still fashionable and a waist-length jacket called a *spencer* and an ankle length coat called a *pelisse* were also designed for outdoor wear.

The heads which topped these long slender forms were small and comparatively neat, the hair being dressed in Greek style with a high coil and a triple bandeau or cut short and worn in curls or little ringlets. Most of the numerous hat and cap styles owed little to antiquity, but a few appeared to be inspired by the helmets worn by Greek and Roman soldiers. Straw was rapidly becoming the most popular material for hats and efforts were being made in England to compete with the fine Italian product by splitting the straw before plaiting it. By 1803 a special splitter had been invented for the purpose.

The simple classical style of dress became gradually modified between 1810 and 1820; the skirts were shorter revealing the feet and wider at the hem, whilst the sleeves were growing larger. The high-crowned, wide-brimmed bonnet was very fashionable.

From 1820 and 1836 another complete change took place in women's appearance, a kind of prelude to the elaborate costume of the Victorian era. Clothes seemed to be influenced by fashions of the past, particularly those of the sixteenth and seventeenth centuries. The waistline returned to its natural position and was once more encouraged to become extremely small. Skirts were shortened to ankle length and were gathered or pleated into a belt. By means of stiffening and petticoats a cone shape was achieved reminiscent of the Tudor period. The sleeves were also stiffened, wired or padded to keep the huge puffed shapes which reached maximum size in the early 1830's. A feature of this period was the ruff-like neck trimmings and the frills, ruching, piping or bows which ornamented the hems and sleeves.

The enormous hats of the 1820's and the equally large bonnets which succeeded them seemed to provide the necessary balance for the extreme width at sleeves and hem and to emphasize the romantic quality often associated with this period.

The straw hat industry developed rapidly in England during this century, and due to the increased efforts to improve the fineness of the straw a fine textured Dunstable was becoming an acceptable alternative to Italian *Leghorn* and was, of course, much cheaper.

As far as men's clothes were concerned the influence of English taste became more apparent during the last decade of the eighteenth century and a lead was established in this country which exists to this day. Quality of material and excellence of cut became more important than constant changes in style. The development of the basic costume of jacket and trousers and the increasing use of subdued colours reduced masculine costume to a mere foil or background for the rapidly changing colourful feminine fashions.

Georgian

1 Hairstyles 1790–1810

By the beginning of the 1790's high headdresses had completely gone out of fashion and great masses of curls or ringlets rioted over women's heads and flowed over their shoulders often reaching to the waist as already described. Wide ribbon bandeaux or swathes of gauze were especially fashionable with curly hair (Fig. 197). Soaring ostrich plumes of all colours worn either singly or in groups were particularly favoured for Court and dress wear (Fig. 198). False hair and wigs were still occasionally worn, and pads and cushions were used for the fuller styles. In 1795 a hairdresser in Bond Street advertised *Brunswick fillets*, which he described as "super elegant, sold with curls complete, fit either for morning or full dress, from seven and six to ten and sixpence each, also braids and chignons in eight lengths."

The use of hair powder rapidly declined and a tax imposed on it in 1795 further accelerated this trend, although it made occasional appearances in the early years of the nineteenth century.

As most new styles came from France it was not long before English women were having their back hair cropped *à la victime* or *à la guillotine*, or were adopting the *Titus* cut (Fig. 200). There were many variations of this cropped style. Sometimes the hair was cut short over the front and sides but left long at the back hanging in ringlets or loops.

Those who preferred not to have their hair cut short adopted variations on the Grecian style, with the hair drawn to the back of the head and tied in a bunch of curls or ringlets or arranged in a bun. Pads and false hair were sometimes used to emphasize the elongated shape of this style (Fig. 199).

In February 1797 the *Lady's Magazine* described the fashionable headdress as being dressed low and full or frizzed low upon the forehead, the "hind" hair turned up plain or in a full chignon.

During the early years of the nineteenth century short hair was still popular (Fig. 202), but there was much experimenting with wigs, half-wigs and false curls, chignons, braids, combs, jewels, diadems, ropes of pearls, flowers and feathers. The names given to the various styles of coiffures and wigs, e.g. *à la Sappho, à la Venus, à la Caracalla*, revealed the taste for Greek, Roman and oriental fashions. Fig. 203 shows an example of the style *à l'Egyptienne* which consisted of two rows of beads round the forehead with a comb and ornaments displayed behind the hair which was plaited and coiled in the shape of a corkscrew.

The *Lady's Magazine* in 1800 contains a description of the ladies' headdresses on the occasion of the King's birthday celebrations: ". . . the hair was dressed in the Grecian style without powder, to show the back of the neck and fastened with combs of diamonds, gold, etc. There was scarcely a lady without a wreath of diamonds or pearls; some caps richly spangled and trimmed with Vandykes were worn. Several paradise plumes also appeared. Bandeaux were much worn and a profusion of feathers, diamonds, topazes and antiques were general." Another fashionable coiffure seen at a ball consisted of fair hair in ringlets to the neck and combed down on the forehead with a wreath of red roses passing obliquely over the head and a band of gold entwined with one of rose coloured satin.

White wigs, or at least a braid of white tresses, were recommended for undress or morning wear as they give "an air of youth".

Continental fashion comments reveal that an appearance of casualness was carefully cultivated. "The bonnet—worn very much on one side of the head so as to discover the hair carelessly curled"; or "the hair chiefly worn in dishevelled ends, exhibiting much of the forehead."

Fig. 197 *c.* 1795

Fig. 198 1799

Fig. 199 1802

Fig. 200 1796

Fig. 201 1806

Fig. 202 1805

Fig. 203 1806

Georgian

2 Caps 1790–1810

In the mid-1790's indoor caps became less fashionable, although small mobs might be worn in the morning or occasionally under hats. For "full dress", however, some kind of headdress or cap was considered almost essential, and allowing for occasional disappearances from the fashionable scene the turban in some shape or form was by far the most popular form of indoor headwear throughout this period.

In 1800 the *Lady's Magazine* announced that turbans were no longer the mode, but in 1802 they were apparently as fashionable as ever. They were made in all kinds of fine material of the kind then fashionable for dresses, such as crepe, muslin, tulle, lace, silk, and gold or silver net. In the 1790's tall ostrich feathers were as popular for turbans as they were for all headwear **(Fig. 204)**, but by the beginning of the nineteenth century aigrettes were more usual, and in some cases rather lavish trimming was advocated. In 1806 a fashionable full-dress turban was trimmed with "a rosette of lace and ornamented gold-spangled net, an aigrette in front, with a large row of muslin confining the whole and a row of gold intermixed with rosette lace and spangled net hanging tastefully to one side of the forehead." In the same year an opera cap consisting of a lace veil formed into a kind of turban, with a wreath of half-dead laurel leaves, an hyacinth in the middle, edged over the forehead with swansdown and a handsome comb behind the head was considered particularly elegant! However, many headdresses were comparatively simple, such as the *trencher* cap of crimson silk with pearls intended for wearing to the opera **(Fig. 208)** and the *Circassian* turban of silver lamé trimmed with a bird of paradise plume **(Fig. 209)**.

Towards the end of this period caps, especially if made of lace were considered essential with morning dress and small round ones were much in evidence **(Fig. 207)**. Ribbon trimmings were more fashionable than feathers or flowers. Veils of muslin or lace, or half handkerchiefs were sometimes draped over the head as an alternative to other forms of headdress especially in hot weather **(Fig. 205)**.

Fig. 205 1801

Fig. 204 1795

Fig. 206 1802

Fig. 207 1805

Fig. 208 1806

Fig. 209 1806

Georgian

3 Hats 1790–1800

Several of the fashionable hat styles of the 1780's continued until about 1794, especially the tall-crowned variety and those with soft crowns, but the vogue for short hair and classical styles soon transformed fashionable hats and they all became as small as previously they had been large.

Fig. 210 illustrates a bonnet of satin and tulle, intended for wear with a walking dress, which might be described as transitional between the large soft crowned hats of the 1780's and the smaller hats of the 1790's. The distinction between bonnets and hats is still difficult to discern at this period.

Riding hats were usually of black beaver and were either of the tall-crowned variety or had round crowns with narrow or tricorne brims. Hat bands and feathers were the usual decoration **(Fig. 211)**.

The straw or bergère hat **(Fig. 212)** persisted in popularity, although the brim was smaller and the crown sometimes disappeared altogether, the hat being held in place by ribbon or a length of material taken over the top and tied under the chin. A rival to this hat was the *poking* hat or bonnet **(Fig. 213)** which made its appearance towards the end of the century and was the forerunner of the most popular form of headwear of the nineteenth century. Another version of this style had a round crown fitting the head, whilst the brim, non-existent at the back, jutted out in front like an exaggerated peak.

The turban hat was another favourite form of headgear. The beret type **(Fig. 214)**, was to reach its zenith of popularity in the Regency period. Long or short veils of net, muslin or other delicate material were often draped over the smaller hats.

Fig. 210 1795

Fig. 211 1793

Fig. 212 1795

Fig. 213 1797

Fig. 214 1798

Georgian

4 Hats 1800–1810

By 1800 small round or oval hats were almost universally worn, the former being suitable for the short hairstyles whilst the latter fitted comfortably over the Grecian coiffures (**Figs 215 and 216**). Both these hats were made of straw which, regardless of season, was now immensely popular for hats worn with morning dress. Openwork and "patent perforated" Leghorn and chip hats, striped straw and coloured chip, especially yellow, were popular in the first three years of the century. Hats made of satin were fashionable for full dress (**Fig. 217**).

By the middle of the decade a bewildering variety of hats and bonnets was available to adorn the heads of the fashion conscious. "It is utterly impossible to describe what is most fashionable," wrote a contributor to *La Belle Assemblée* in 1806, "a lady is not considered fashionable if she appears in public for two successive days in the same bonnet." Every style and variation had a name, either topical or fanciful. The *Trafalgar* and *military* bonnets vied for favour with the *Nelson*, *conversation* and *mistake* hats. A lingering yearning for the simple country life was suggested by such names as the *yeoman* and *woodland* hat or the *mountain* or *cottage* bonnet. A distinction was now becoming apparent between hats and bonnets, the latter being brimless or having a brim only round the front. They were not as yet always tied with ribbons under the chin. **Fig. 218** shows a *jockey* bonnet which was made of lilac-coloured silk with a long lace veil hanging almost to the knees. Large veils of lace-edged net were now becoming popular. These were carelessly thrown over the hat either to cover the face or to form drapery round the neck.

Modified versions of the popular country straw tied round with a ribbon, kerchief or scarf still appeared frequently, and were known by a variety of names. The example in **Fig. 221** was known as the *gypsy* and another version of this style known as the *Village* hat had the brim turned up sharply at front and back echoing the

style of the 1750's. The *Lavinia* or *Witch's* hat in which the brim and crown were formed in a similar way to a Chinese *coolie* hat was also fashionable. Larger brims were beginning to appear by 1806. Trimmings were generally fairly restrained and consisted mainly of ribbons, feathers or artificial flowers, straw being sometimes used for the latter.

It was fashionable for hats and bonnets to match mantles and pelisses, for example a Russian mantle of fawn coloured kersey-mere was worn with a turban hat of the same material, or a hat made of figured jonquil green Chinese silk matched a coat of similar material (**Fig. 220**).

In winter caps and hats were often trimmed with fur to match similar edging on robes and coats, but a wide range of materials was used both for the hats and for their trimmings.

Fig. 215 1800

Fig. 216 1801

Fig. 217 1802

Fig. 218 1802

Fig. 219 1805

Fig. 220 1808

Fig. 221 1806

Georgian

5 Hairstyles 1810–1837

During the early years of this period the classical and short styles began to give place gradually to the elaborate curls and ringlets, the masses of hair, either sleek or waved, which were to adorn women's heads for the next hundred years. At first the small wisps of hair and little curls on the forehead and temples were allowed to grow longer whilst the rest of the hair tended to be dressed towards the crown of the head. Flower ornaments, a French fashion, were worn for evening (**Fig. 222**). Gradually the front hair became more important and was arranged in a mass of small curls, the back hair meanwhile being twisted or plaited into a large top knot (**Fig. 223**). By the mid-1820's the top knot had developed into an arrangement of glossily smooth bows, loops and braids requiring skilful dressing with wire frames and special pins. As the coiffures became more complicated further ornaments were added such as feathers, pearls, ribbons, ears of wheat and flowers, the latter also being wired in order to make them stand erect. The loops or *coques* of hair were often known as *Apollo* knots particularly when the tresses were twisted or swathed round at the base (**Fig. 225**). Details of these fashionable styles *à la giraffe* changed constantly. Another style, *à la chinoise* was one in which the hair was drawn up tightly into a coil or plait on top of the head and kept in place by long pins with ornamental heads called *Glauvina* pins. These pins were also used for other styles, and high combs of tortoiseshell or gilt metal set with jewels were also worn. Black hair was admired at this time and alarming recipes were suggested for obtaining dark shades. In 1830 readers of Godey's *Lady's Book* were recommended "to wash the hair daily with warm soft water to which, occasionally a portion of soap will be a very proper addition." Other writers, however, strongly disapproved of wetting the hair, maintaining that many evil consequences were likely to follow.

By 1835 the hairstyles had become lower and less elaborate. The fantastic loops of hair were transformed into a coiled or braided knot set high at the back of the head. The hair was parted in various ways, either in the centre or with a short centre parting for the front hair only. Alternatively, partings might be made on either side of the head with the top brushed straight back or parted in two short diagonals in a V shape with the point towards the forehead. The clusters of curls became longer and fell in corkscrew ringlets (**Fig. 227**). These coiffures, *à la Vandyck* as they were called, were inspired by those in seventeenth-century portraits. Sometimes the ringlets were discarded in favour of a flat, sleek styling with a centre parting *à la Madonna*. Both arrangements were the forerunners of the demure early Victorian styles.

Fig. 222 1815

Fig. 223 1820

Fig. 224 1823

Fig. 225 1829

Fig. 226 1830

Fig. 227 1835

Georgian

6 Caps and turbans 1810–1837

The first ten years or so of this period showed the continuing popularity of caps and turbans. At first the round or elongated oval shaped persisted (**Fig. 228**), but as the hairstyles became higher so the caps and other headwear grew upwards in order to accommodate them. As a rule caps continued to be worn for indoor day wear, but the material of which they were made seemed to be a determining factor in deciding when they might be worn. In the early 1820's mob caps and cornettes (caps with rounded or pointed cauls and fastened under the chin) were, for morning wear, made of muslin embroidered or trimmed with lace. For half dress, that is, more formal occasions lace, fine net, satin or coloured crepe was used and ribbon or flowers were sometimes added, especially for dinner parties (**Fig. 232**). In the late 1820's morning cornettes were made of figured fine net or thread lace with bows of striped or chequered ribbon. The lappets were left unfastened. Small caps of blond (lace) sometimes had cauls made of coloured silk or tartan. During this decade caps were frequently worn under bonnets but never under hats. The elaborate arrangement of the hair caused many caps to be made without cauls whilst others had openings to admit the "coques" of hair. By the mid-'thirties the tendency for the ears to be covered made long lappets very fashionable. **Fig. 233** shows a dinner cap with a high crown known as the *babet* style. This example was made of tulle trimmed with lace-edged net and bows of ribbon.

For evening, toques made of satin or velvet (**Fig. 229**), and turbans of elaborate form and increasingly large size were worn throughout the period (**Fig. 231**). These headdresses were given names as fanciful as their styles and were made in all kinds of materials, silk, satin, velvet, gold and silver tissue, gauze and cotton. Striped materials were particularly popular and sometimes two or three different fabrics were used together. Trimmings consisted of feathers, gold or silver fringes, cords, tassels, pearls and brooches. Scarves and handkerchiefs were also made up into headdresses. A *madras* turban consisted of a silk or cotton handkerchief, patterned in bright colours such as blue and orange, tied like a bandanna and fastened with a flower or brooch on the top left-hand side. A style which came down on the forehead in a point was introduced in 1823 and appeared at intervals throughout the next decade (**Fig. 230**). Throughout the 1820's, however, the turbans were rivalled by the large hats and increasingly came to be worn only by older women. In 1827 it was noted in *La Belle Assemblée* that beret turbans to match their dresses were much worn by matrons, and in 1834 *The Ladies' Magazine* stated that turbans were fashionable for chaperons. The following year the same magazine informed its readers that "turbans continue in undiminished favour, those of point lace being the most elegant. They are indispensable headdresses for concerts and at balls for ladies who do not dance." This was evidently a fashion which died slowly.

Fig. 228 1813

Fig. 229 1817

Fig. 230 1828

Fig. 231 1831

Fig. 232 1830

Fig. 233 1836

Georgian

7 Bonnets 1810–1837

During the first two or three years of this period small styles of headwear continued to be fashionable, with the bonnet gradually increasing in popularity. From about 1812 the crown became higher in order to accommodate the rising hairstyles and the brim, although small at first, became wider, forming a sweeping open curve round the face (**Figs 234** and **235**). Until the early 1820's all kinds of fancy bonnets were fashionable and they were made in a variety of materials such as satin, crêpe and *gros de Naples*, but velvet and straw were the most generally used. Trimmings of feathers, ribbon, and pleated, ruched or puffed fabric adorned the bonnets and decorative large veils of lace, embroidered net or figured gauze were often worn draped over the sides and back. Small *cornettes* were frequently worn beneath the bonnets, with the frilled edges showing.

Between about 1824 and 1831 the popularity of the bonnet was challenged by the hat, and although it was acceptable for day wear it was not considered high fashion during the late 'twenties. Like the hats of this time it developed to an immense size, the sweeping curves of the brim being stiffened with iron wire or whalebone and the *bavolet* made an occasional appearance. This was a small curtain, attached to the brimless back of the bonnet, which was soon to become an essential feature of this type of headwear. It sometimes appeared on hats also, but then a brim was always present beneath. Broad ribbons were attached under the brim, but were often left floating loose and the crown and brim were lavishly trimmed with flowers, feathers and bows or loops of ribbon which were often wired to stand erect (**Fig. 236**). In 1827 a yellow silk bonnet sent into the country to a lady of high rank carried such an enormous quantity of ribbon that each loop of every separate bow required half an ell (one and a quarter yards). Bonnets made of materials such as silk or satin had the brims lined with similar fabric over an interlining of stiff muslin or net. Brims of straw

bonnets were not usually lined but the high crowns were sometimes reinforced by a lining of cardboard.

From 1831 onwards the bonnet or *capote*, as it was often called, became extremely fashionable. It was now somewhat reduced in size, although it tended to remain quite large until the end of the decade. The most fashionable style had a brim of oval shape whilst the crown tended to remain high, often attaining an almost perpendicular position (**Fig. 238**), but as the hairstyles became lower so the crowns were reduced in height. The wearing of a cap beneath the bonnet was discontinued and instead flowers, ribbons, lace and ruchings or puffs of material were attached to the underside of the brim (**Fig. 239**). One of the several variations in bonnet styles was the *bibi* or cottage bonnet which was to become the universal fashion during the next decade. This was a style which particularly appealed to the Englishwoman and was popular amongst all classes. The *drawn* bonnet was another important type particularly fashionable in 1835 and which continued to be worn throughout the next period. This was made of fine material gathered over a series of cane hoops in a manner resembling the eighteenth-century calash and could be adapted to conform in shape to any prevailing fashion. It is interesting to note that small calashes existed in this period also and were probably worn to protect the elaborate hairstyles in wet or windy weather.

As a fair complexion was considered attractive large veils were often worn with the more fashionable high-brimmed bonnets, particularly in summer. Like the headwear of the previous period bonnet styles were often named after events or famous personalities such as Blücher, Oldenburg, Valois and Cambridge.

In the 1830's riding was a popular pastime. Hats varied from the high *top hat* to low crowned *cavalier* or cap styles. Brims of top hats were usually narrow with trimmings of feathers and green gauze veiling (**Fig. 237**).

Fig. 234 1816

Fig. 235 1817

Fig. 236 1830

Fig. 237 1834

Fig. 238 1835

Fig. 239 1835

Georgian

8 Hats 1810–1837

About 1820 a style of bonnet appeared which showed a downward dip in the centre front of the brim (**Fig. 240**). Within a short time this curve had become flattened and although the ribbons were still sometimes tied under the chin they were often allowed to hang loose so that the sides of the brim were no longer held close to the cheeks. These two features were the stages whereby the bonnet became transformed once more into the hat. Once established the hat grew larger and by the middle of the 1820's had reached an enormous size and was decorated with huge bows and loops of wide ribbon or with sprays of flowers and leaves, ears of corn and similar ornaments branching out in every direction. In 1826 *La Belle Assemblée* described both hats and bonnets as "monstrous", adding that "the size of Leghorns is immense and the puffings of silk and ribbon add to their dimensions". Ostrich feathers were also favourite ornaments, especially for evening wear. These large hats became so fashionable that they were worn for every occasion, including dinner parties and the opera where they made any sight of the stage an impossibility for those unfortunate enough to be seated behind the wearers. **Fig. 242** shows one of these hats intended for evening wear and made of white transparent crêpe with a fluting under the brim of wide blond and trimmed with white plumes. The ribbons of pink satin to match the dress were long enough to reach the knees. These floating ribbons, several inches in width, were one feature of the bonnet which was retained on many of the hats. They were attached to the underside of the brim or one above and one below as in **Fig. 243**.

Leghorn and Dunstable straw were much used for hats as well as for bonnets, but other materials such as velvet were used. In the summer of 1826 hats of transparent material were fashionable and also cotton hats which were claimed to be washable. All hats were worn with a slight downward curve from right to left and tilted towards the back of the head to allow for the fashionable clusters of curls.

By 1829 the hat was beginning to be worn still further back on the head with the brim tilted up in front, and when the ribbons were attached to the outside of the brim it was on the way to becoming a bonnet once more. By 1834 it had virtually disappeared.

Fig. 240 1824

Fig. 241 1829

Fig. 242 1827

Fig. 243 1828

Early Victorian
1837–1860

Throughout the whole of the nineteenth century women's costume showed rapid changes of style, but few of the designs were truly original, most of them being based on ideas from the past. With few exceptions the fashions derived from Paris. Well-to-do women in the leading European countries were able to follow the latest trends by reading the numerous women's journals with hand-coloured fashion plates which were published during the period.

In the course of the Victorian era the development of industry produced a middle class enjoying considerable wealth and importance. The ideals and virtues of this class permeated much of Victorian society and its attitudes affected the development of costume. The conservative style of men's dress now became firmly established and was accepted as appropriate for the head of a family devoting himself to the serious business of making money. The early Victorian woman was looked upon with sentimentality as elegant and refined, modest and virtuous. With plenty of servants to do her bidding she was not expected or indeed thought capable of any kind of work. The clothes she wore were designed to express this masculine view of her. The element of sexual attraction was also evident in the close-fitting bodices and tiny waists and for evening wear the very low necklines revealing the shoulders. The small waist was a feature of women's dress throughout the whole of the Victorian era and was accompanied inevitably by corsets and tight lacing. The bodice of the day dress had a high neck finished by a demure collar and the tight sleeves were set into low armholes below the shoulder line. The full skirt was attached to the bodice in deep pleats or fine gathers forming a bell shape which swept the ground. Ankles were now completely hidden, but a glimpse was permitted of tiny feet clad in tight-fitting cloth bootees. During the 'forties and 'fifties the skirts grew wider, requiring more and more petticoats to support them until the introduction of the crinoline enabled women to dispense with the great masses of material and gave them more freedom of movement. At the same time the light metal framework of the new invention made it possible to have skirts of even greater circumference, their apparent width being further increased by several tiers of deep flounces. These huge round skirts and the quantities of material, lace and trimmings which were used gave an even more static quality to the general appearance and enhanced the impression of woman as a decorative symbol of her husband's affluence. Sleeves remained close fitting at the shoulders but increased considerably in width at the elbows, echoing the shape of the skirts. For outdoor wear shawls and caped mantles were popular. Various types of short or three-quarter length jackets were also worn, usually hanging loose. These features of the costume added to the pyramidal feminine shape which was further emphasized by the small neat heads enclosed in decorative little bonnets.

The straw bonnet, formerly worn only by ladies of fashion, was now within the reach of all classes due to the expansion of the English straw plaiting and hat manufacturing industry which reached its peak of production in the middle decades of the nineteenth century. Italian plait continued to be imported for use in better-class work as the Italians were able constantly to design new and delicate patterns. This plait was expensive but hats made from it could be re-blocked and re-sewn to last a number of seasons. Cheaper bonnets and hats were made of English plait or the somewhat inferior Chinese rice straw or *canton* plait. Straws of all kinds, wheat, rice, barley and also grasses were plaited into an enormous variety of designs. Cotton, silk and crin (horsehair) were also used to produce delicately patterned braids resembling lace which were sewn together in a similar manner to straw plaits. Until the invention of suitable sewing machines in the 1870's the plait had to be sewn by hand. This was a highly skilled process as the stitching had to be concealed beneath the narrow rows of plait working outwards from the centre of the crown whilst shaping the bonnet at the same time. It was then blocked by hand and stiffened with gelatine.

The introduction of aniline dyes in 1856 made it possible to produce plait in a greater variety of shades and with a better finish than had been possible with vegetable dyes. Coloured and bleached straws were often combined to make speckled plaits.

Early Victorian

1 Hairstyles 1837–1860

By the beginning of Queen Victoria's reign hairstyles had undergone an almost complete transformation from those of the early 'thirties. The hair was flat on top and usually parted in the centre and drawn smoothly back to a knot or bun which was sometimes as high as the crown but usually lower. Side interest was still shown in various ways, one of the most popular being the arrangement of side curls or long ringlets (Fig. 244). This style, whilst it was a natural development of that of a decade or so earlier, was reminiscent of the fashions of the court of Charles I, a period in which there was great interest at this time.

Another method of arrangement was to make a central parting in the front hair only and to draw the two strands in smooth loops or in one or more braids down the sides of the cheeks and under the ears (Fig. 245). This style, known as *Agnes Sorel* or *à la Clothilde* was introduced in the early 1830's but did not appear to be popular until some years later. During the mid-'forties braids were frequently adopted, either at the back of the head or in various coronet arrangements over the top. For evening wear feathers, flowers, lace, artificial grapes, etc., were arranged either to encircle the head or were attached to the side or back of the head (Fig. 246). Long hair became more and more admired and quantities of hair began to be imported from abroad in order that women might supplement their own.

During the 'fifties ringlets became less usual but braids continued to be worn and hair was plaited in a variety of ways (Fig. 247). The front of the hair was invariably smooth, covering the ears, and was arranged with the intention of emphasizing or creating the illusion of an oval shape. The prevailing fashion of the bonnet and the almost universal wearing of indoor caps during this period necessitated a simple arrangement of the hair, at least during the day. About 1854 a lightly waved effect for the front hair became fashionable (Fig. 248), and a few women began wearing the chignon and hair net, but the majority of women wore their hair in the demure smooth style usually associated with this period (Fig. 249).

Towards the end of the decade there was a gradual shift of interest to the back of the head, which was emphasized by the introduction of the *comb concealer* or *cache peigne*. This was designed to conceal joins or spaces in the coils or braids and consisted of about three yards of velvet or taffeta ribbon made into several loops hanging down behind and attached to a piece of stiff net. Sometimes lace was mixed with the ribbon or was used alone (Fig. 249). The whole was kept in place by ribbon wire curving over the crown of the head. When the cache peigne was used to surround a small braid or twist instead of crossing the back of the head it was held in place by a cap spring or hair pins. For evening wear or dinner parties the cache peigne might consist of flowers, or mixtures of flowers, pearls, lace and ribbon, but ornaments of all kinds were also worn, including fancy combs and feathers.

Fig. 244 1844

Fig. 245 1841

Fig. 246 1845

Fig. 247 1854

Fig. 248 1855

Fig. 249 1858

Early Victorian

2 Caps 1837–1860

A great variety of caps and headdresses was worn during the Victorian era and especially during the early and middle periods. The wearing of caps varied considerably during the course of the reign, but throughout the early period the tendency was for nearly every woman to wear a cap suited to the occasion or time of day, be it night, morning or evening. Night caps, which were generally worn until about 1880, were almost always rather plain and the style changed only slightly between 1835 and 1870. They were usually made of lawn or muslin, with frills and perhaps insertions of openwork embroidery or narrow lace, or were sometimes knitted or crocheted in cotton. **Fig. 252** shows the usual shape of the cap, which fitted closely to the head with a drawstring across the back. This example belonged to Queen Victoria and was perhaps rather more elaborate than the usual run of such caps. The size of night caps tended to become smaller as the period progressed.

The plainer types of morning cap resembled the night caps, but were made of finer quality material and were trimmed with lace and insertions of embroidery. The more elaborate ones were made of lace, or of net with lace-trimmed frills, and insertions of lace or embroidery. Occasionally a heavier material such as satin might be used, but the lighter fabrics were more usual. Additional trimmings were of silk or gauze ribbon, either coloured or patterned, which formed bows or hanging lappets. Small round caps were also made of netted or crocheted cotton with long lappets over the ears. It was unusual for morning caps to be tied under the chin. Considerable quantities of material were required for the trimming and borders of many caps. In 1847 it was suggested that goffered frills might require five to seven yards of fabric and for trimming three to 12 yards of ribbon according to width. Cap styles tended to follow those of the bonnet. In the 1830's they had been worn high at the back of the head with round cauls and wide frills framing the face. Later the frills and trimmings were arranged at the sides of the head covering the ears (**Fig. 253**). By the mid-1840's the cap shape fitted more closely to the head, forming a horizontal line from front to back as in the morning cap illustrated in **Fig. 254**. In the 1850's caps became smaller and like the bonnets were worn towards the back of the head, exposing much of the front hair. "Dress" caps also followed the close fitting style of bonnets during the 1840's and early 1850's and were made of delicate materials such as net, silk, gauze and lace, "blond" being still fashionable for them at the beginning of this period. Sometimes alternate bands of ribbon and lace or insertions of embroidery and lace were used. Trimmings of flowers, feathers or knots of ribbon were placed at the sides over the ears. Generally speaking, the grander the occasion the less covering was worn on the head. Throughout the period coronets of flowers or of velvet trimmed with lace, beads or straw ornaments were worn with evening dress by younger women.

A popular style during this period, especially for morning wear was the *fanchon* or kerchief cap which had been first introduced in 1837. It consisted of a piece of material, usually triangular or occasionally square in shape, resting on top of the head with one point worn towards the front, and with bows and streamers behind or lappets on either side. A single shaped piece of lace or embroidery with ends covering the ears was another version of the style (**Fig. 251**) and the fashionable morning cap shown in **Fig. 255** was yet another example.

During the early years of the period turban-style headdresses were still worn for evening by some older women and young matrons, but many headdresses described as turbans were made of narrow gauze or lace scarves arranged in puffs and folds or twisted into the coils of hair leaving most of the head uncovered. **Fig. 250** shows an example of this type of headdress worn with a forehead ornament or *ferronière* which had been in vogue since the beginning of the century.

By the late 1850's younger fashionable women had ceased to wear caps and tended instead to wear slighter forms of headdress such as the cache peigne which were linked with the fashionable style of hairdressing.

Fig. 250 1840

Fig. 251 1840–1850

Fig. 252 1840–1850

Fig. 253 1840

Fig. 254 1845

Fig. 255 1853

Early Victorian

3 Bonnets 1837–1860

The bonnet was the most characteristic form of feminine headwear in the nineteenth century and during the Early Victorian period was not merely popular but was considered to be the only correct form of outdoor head covering except for the most informal occasions. During the late 1830's the capote bonnet was almost universally worn, but the brim was becoming smaller and more circular in shape whilst the high crown was now no longer needed to accommodate an elaborate hairstyle (**Fig. 256**).

The first real change in the shape of the bonnet showed a return to the type which had been worn at the beginning of the century and which was also known as the *bibi* or cottage bonnet. A distinguishing feature of this form of bonnet and the variations which developed during the course of the period was the continuous line formed by the crown and the brim. During the whole of the 1840's this bonnet was worn straight, the lower edge of the brim curving down from the back of the crown to cover the cheeks. In the close style the brim curved in such a way as to hide almost completely the wearer's profile (**Figs 257** and **259**). There was another version of this style of bonnet in which the brim opened more widely round the face (**Fig. 260**). This latter style became more generally worn, and during the early 1850's it developed into a new shape which was worn well towards the back of the head. The crown was smaller and the brim, instead of demurely shading the wearer's face, now opened widely to reveal the front of the head (**Fig. 261**).

During the last years of the decade the brim of the bonnet came forward onto the forehead, but still curved back on either side (**Fig. 262**). All bonnets were tied beneath the chin with broad ribbons and had a curtain hanging from the back. This bavolet was usually of similar material to the bonnet and on the small styles of the 'fifties, it was often very long. Many different fabrics were used for making the bonnets, velvet being the most popular for winter and straw for the summer. For "dress" wear they might be made of different kinds of silk, either plain, figured or watered, or they might be of the *transparent* type made of rows of lace or folds of gauze and similar delicate material arranged over foundations of Paris net or frames of silk wire. The "drawn" bonnet construction was also still in use (**Fig. 258**).

The trimmings of bonnets during this period consisted of ribbons, feathers and flowers and tended to be concentrated at the sides. The inside of the brim was considered just as important as the outside for not only was it lined, but also profusely trimmed with frills of lace or ruchings of net, flowers and ribbons to form a frame for the face. In addition, the earlier type of bonnet sometimes had a veil draped over.

Fig. 256 1840

Fig. 257 1845

Fig. 258 1845–1850

Fig. 259 1848

Fig. 260 1850

Fig. 261 1855

Fig. 262 1859

Early Victorian

4 Hats 1837–1860

At the beginning of the reign hats were quite out of fashion, the bonnet being considered the only proper outdoor headwear for any lady. Indeed, throughout almost the whole of this period hats appeared only in the garden or on the most informal occasions in the country or at the seaside. As might be expected they were of straw and were usually low crowned with wide brims sweeping into upward curves on either side. Another style called *Diana Vernon* had the brim turned up at one side. From about 1857 hats became fashionable for younger women, but still only for informal wear. These, too, were low crowned, with curving brims which were often bound with ribbon, and had broad ribbons hanging from the back or from each side. For country and seaside straw was still the most usual material, although other fabrics were beginning to be used. For example in 1858 garden hats of white muslin were very fashionable. Other materials such as plush or silk were used for hats for carriage or promenade wear. They were trimmed around the crown or under the brim with ribbon puffs and flowers and the broad ribbons on either side might be tied in a bow under the chin but were more often allowed to float freely. Very often a long feather curved round the crown and a curtain of lace often several inches deep was attached to the edge of the brim (**Fig. 264**).

Another hat which appeared about 1860 and became extremely popular was the small round *pork pie* style. It was worn tilted forward and was often trimmed with a tuft of small feathers (**Fig. 267**).

Riding hats were generally of the top hat style with floating green veils (**Fig. 263**).

For evening wear, in addition to the turban, caps and other headdresses, there was a fashion for little hats called *Petits Bords*. The interest shown in historical personages was reflected in many of the designs and in the names given to these headdresses. The one illustrated in **Fig. 265** called *Bord à la Marie Stuart* was described

as being made of white tulle with lappets of white lace arranged in loops and ends.

Fig. 266 shows a hood or *capulet* which was described as being made of cashmere lined with silk and edged with narrow black velvet. This was designed to be worn at the seaside, presumably for windy or cool weather. Another article of headwear made its appearance at the seaside during this period. This was a curious contraption related to the eighteenth-century calash, which was attached to the front of bonnets in order to protect the complexion from the sun. The *ugly*, as it was known, was made of silk, usually blue, gathered over several half-hoops of cane, and could be folded into a single half-hoop when not required. The ends had ribbon ties which may have been fastened under the chin or more likely were passed round the back of the bonnet underneath the curtain and tied there or at the side (**Fig. 268**). The *ugly* continued in use until the 1860's.

Fig. 263 1840

Fig. 264 1858

Fig. 265 1849

Fig. 266 1858

Fig. 267 1860

Fig. 268 1854

Mid-Victorian
1860–1880

The vast crinoline skirts remained fashionable until about 1865 and continued to be popular with many women for several years. The wide bell-shaped sleeves were replaced by *pagoda* sleeves widely flaring in tiers of frills to match those on the skirts. The dress fabrics were heavy and contrasting materials were combined by means of bands or inset vertical strips, whilst trimmings of lace, braid, ruching, frills and fringes were lavishly applied. Since the discovery of aniline dyes much use was made of harsh colours and clashing combinations of these colours were often worn.

In the late 'sixties a gradual change took place in the shape of the skirt. The front and sides became somewhat flattened, but a considerable projection remained at the back and interest was to be centred on this area for more than 20 years. A revival of an earlier eighteenth-century fashion, the polonaise, led to the combination of the tight-fitting bodice with an overskirt of half or three-quarter length open down the front. This overskirt was looped up or bunched towards the back and the mass of material was supported on the shaped back portion of the crinoline and became known as the bustle. A simpler method of forming the bustle consisted of an arrangement of horsehair pads tied on beneath the underskirt with tapes around the waist. Bodice necklines were high and sleeves resembled those of coats with lace frills at the wrist. The fashion for the bustle was fairly short lived and by 1875 the size was less obvious and the line of the skirt at the back was long and gently sloping. The bodice formed an extremely smooth and close fitting sheath from shoulder to hip, whilst the skirt appeared to give little room for leg movement— the yards of drapery which had formed the bustle were now arranged in complicated folds and twists somewhere behind the knees, extending into a train or fan-like "tail". Softer darker colours were more generally favoured during the 'seventies, but dresses in two contrasting colours or with contrasting trimmings were still extremely popular. Yards of material were needed for dresses, especially for grand ball gowns—almost every garment was edged with rows of frills.

The hairstyles of this period make an interesting comparison with the back views of the skirts. The large chignons of the early 'sixties echoed the growing projection at the rear of the figure and the piled up curls and cascades of ringlets repeated the draperies of the bustle and the skirts of the late 'seventies.

Although fashionable clothes were elaborate and overloaded with fussy decoration various factors were at work gradually bringing about a change in women's dress. A century earlier Englishwomen had been influential in the move towards simpler styles and now they showed a preference for less formal clothes, especially for outdoor wear. A taste for travel which grew with the expansion of the railways spread to all classes, and week-end excursions to the seaside or the country were becoming customary for the working population of the industrial towns. Those who could afford to do so spent holidays each year in the country or on the coast, or travelled abroad to the watering places and fashionable tourist resorts of Europe. Ideas of female emancipation were beginning to stir and young women were taking up sports such as skating, tennis and cycling. These trends helped to encourage the development of clothing which allowed greater mobility and one of the first signs of this was the appearance of a shorter walking skirt revealing the feet and ankles. A comparatively loose-fitting morning house dress made of lightweight material also appeared at this time. A similar garment for afternoon wear was adopted in England a few years later, where it was known as the tea gown. It provided a pleasant change from the heavy tight-fitting street clothes and elaborate evening dresses. The idea of having clothing designed for every occasion and for different times of day was one which gained ground as the nineteenth century progressed. A fashionable woman who lived a busy social life needed an extensive wardrobe and might have to change her dress several times in one day.

The improvement in the domestic sewing machine enabled many to make garments at home. The materials to make them, as well as ready-made clothes in all styles and sizes, were becoming available in the large department stores now becoming established in many cities.

Mid-Victorian

1 Hairstyles 1860–1880

The movement of interest from the sides to the back of the head, apparent in the hair arrangement of the late 1850's, was firmly established by 1860. Usually parted in the centre and drawn back smoothly, the hair was plaited or coiled into a large roll known as a *chignon* (**Fig. 270**), which was at first set low on the nape of the neck and often confined in a net. Before long it became fashionable for the chignons to be very large, and the increasing size and variety of styles often necessitated the use of artificial hair made up professionally. Waved hair had been highly fashionable for some years, and among the various methods of achieving this were patent hair wavers which the advertisers claimed would completely and permanently wave the hair in three minutes! They were formed of two sets of curved grooves over one of which the hair was placed, and the undulations were impressed by the other. Dark hair was considered desirable and false hair from France and Italy was therefore sought after and those with fair hair were given advice on dyeing it with recipes such as solutions of permanganate of potash.

Towards the middle of the decade the hair began to be dressed higher on the head, with the main mass of the chignon lifted from the nape of the neck and placed on the back of the head (**Fig. 271**). Coils, braids, switches, curls, *water falls, frizettes* and false pieces of every description were now being used. In 1866 *The English-women's Domestic Magazine* told its readers that "such a large quantity of false hair is necessary for the formation of modern coiffures that we think it well to inform our lady readers into the secrets of the fictitious curls, bows, plaits and chignons to be used for each of them." False ringlets cascaded from the crown of the head or were attached singly to one side of the coiffure and lay over the shoulder. Drooping chignons and smooth catogans of hair, wreaths and garlands of flowers were fashionable for evening wear. Flowers were placed on top of the head or long trailing sprays were mixed with the hair or curved down one side of the head tucked in among the large curls (**Fig. 272**). Ladies became expert at wiring the fresh flowers which were often used, although their choice of blooms such as large white lilies seems rather strange.

About 1867 golden and light tinted hair began to be favoured and gold and silver powder was considered particularly elegant in fashionable circles. Artificial hair was imported chiefly from Northern France, Belgium and Germany. German hair, being lighter in colour, was the most valuable and the wholesale price varied from 30 to 60 shillings a pound. The peasant girls from whom the hair was obtained were given trinkets or articles of dress in exchange for their tresses, which might weigh from three-quarters to one and a half pounds.

The Ladies' Treasury in 1868 quoted a writer to *The Times* as saying: "inasmuch as human hair of any fine quality is worth four or five times as much per ounce as silver the temptation to rob the dead . . . is enough to make us uneasy. . . . Almost every woman wears, more or less, false hair, either in the shape of luxuriant locks . . . or in the shape of frizzets, or the foundations for those monstrous excrescences which are deforming the beautiful contours of the head in the shape of chignons." In the same year *The Ladies' Treasury* announced: "the chignon is now rarely seen, never in fashionable life. Curls short and long are in immense favour."

Drooping chignons formed of large *torsades* or loose coils of hair were still being worn during the 'seventies, but in general the hair was dressed high with waves or *frizzles* over the forehead, whilst the back hair, in plaits or large rolls, was often fastened with coronet-like tortoiseshell combs (**Figs 274** and **275**). A few stray curls only were allowed on the neck, but for evening wear especially, long curls or twists of hair continued to be worn and remained fashionable into the next decade (**Fig. 273**). Ornaments such as bows or flowers were placed in front, a little to one side.

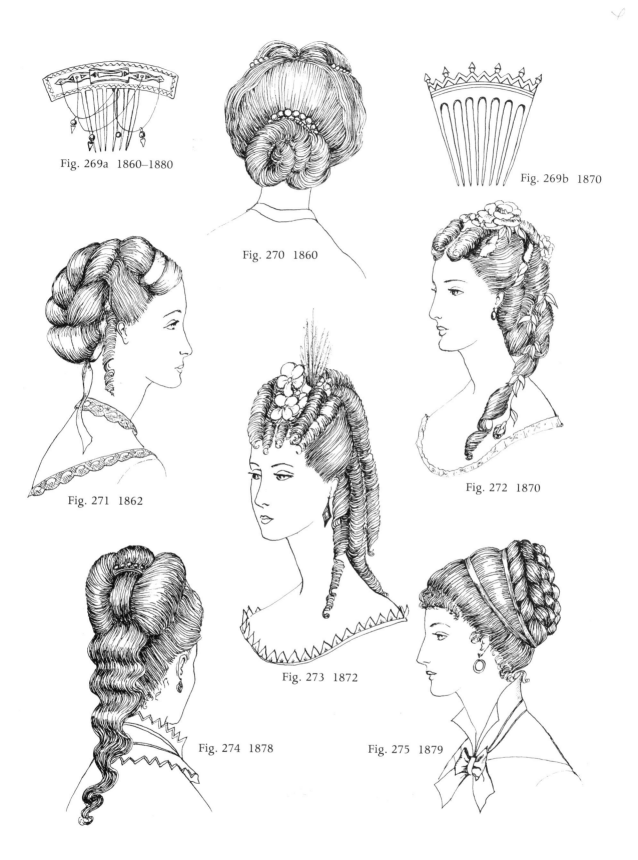

Fig. 269a 1860–1880

Fig. 269b 1870

Fig. 270 1860

Fig. 271 1862

Fig. 272 1870

Fig. 273 1872

Fig. 274 1878

Fig. 275 1879

Mid-Victorian

2 Caps 1860–1880

Caps became fashionable once again during the early years of this period and they were similar in style to the bonnets then being worn. They were usually made of lace or net with a long oval crown and a raised front supported by a light wire frame. The elaborate trimmings were of lace or ribbon (**Fig. 278**). For informal wear the low heavy chignon of hair was often enclosed in a bag-like net. The one in **Fig**. 276 was described as "a headdress of light blue chenille with a blue ribbon and bow—a gold buckle in the centre of the bow. Coiffures of this description are very useful in as much as the hair does not require much dressing." In the late 1860's as the hair was dressed higher the caps changed in style and became flat circles, squares or triangles of net or lace lying across the top of the head. The fanchon or half-kerchief was still popular during this period and occasionally these caps were large enough to hang in folds over the chignon. Cashmere was sometimes used for morning caps and also knitted wool. **Fig.** 277 shows a fanchon made of netted cotton, but lace of all kinds was by far the most fashionable material. Guipure, blond, Honiton, Belgian, Valenciennes and Chantilly were all used. In the 1870's a popular style for morning wear was known as the *Charlotte Corday*. This cap had a round soft crown with lappets or falls of material down the back and trimmings of ribbon and flowers. **Fig.** *279* shows an example made of muslin edged with lace. Another round-crowned cap is shown in **Fig. 281**. The ribbons or lappets might be fastened either under the chignon or under the chin or simply left floating loose. Dress caps were nearly always made of lace and were trimmed with beads, velvet or flowers (**Fig. 280**). By the end of the period they tended to be worn without ribbon ties or lappets.

After 1880 the wearing of dress caps was confined to women past middle age. Morning caps were worn by younger women but gradually the cap as an item of headwear for fashionable women ceased to exist.

Fig. 276 1862

Fig. 277 1866

Fig. 278 1862

Fig. 279 1871

Fig. 280 1872

Fig. 281 1871

Mid-Victorian

3 Bonnets 1860–1880

In the early 1860's the bonnet was still very popular. The fashionable style had a brim curving high above the forehead, the inside was filled with lace and flowers and the crown sloped down towards the back of the head. Fairly large full curtains were usual **(Fig. 282)**. Materials were similar to those used in the previous period, and trimmings were still elaborate. Fruit was in fashion for ornaments in 1860. Although the 20-year-long universal reign of the bonnet was coming to an end its popularity waned slowly and it continued to be worn in a variety of styles until the end of the Victorian period. In 1863 the high front became flatter and the crown smaller. As the coiffure became more elaborate and the hair was piled high on the back of the head the bonnets of necessity became smaller, losing the curtain back whilst the sides receded and disappeared. By the middle of the decade the bonnet was little more than a small light shape of horsehair or lace worn high on the top of the head and by 1870 it was almost indistinguishable from a dress cap, being merely an ornament of ribbon and flowers or a fluting of lace worn towards the front of the head. Small *toques* were worn which were similar to bonnets except that the latter had fairly broad ribbon ties or lappets which were fastened loosely across the throat **(Fig. 283)**.

From 1873 the bonnets were large enough to cover the high chignon and were worn with a slightly backward tilt. One of the popular styles of the 1870's was one with a brim of diadem form and a round crown. The example illustrated in **Fig. 286** was made of cream-coloured straw, the brim ornamented with a double garland of loops of blue ribbon and the crown trimmed with white heather. The ribbon encircling the neck was called a *collier*.

During the middle years of the decade many bonnets were worn without ribbon ties, but both bonnets and hats often had ribbons hanging from the back and both were lavishly trimmed with flowers, feathers and lace. In 1873 the

Milliner and Dressmaker stated that "Chapeau was a better name than bonnet or hat which were by now hardly distinguishable. The bonnet was possibly more dressy and elaborately trimmed, the hat less overloaded with flowers and more suitable for travelling and country wear." From this we can say that the "chapeaux" illustrated in **Fig. 284** and **Fig. 285** may be classed as bonnets. The former, made of rose-coloured silk and trimmed with black velvet ribbon and roses, was a fashionable style with a round crown and brim turned up all round. The second "chapeau" was made of Belgian straw, trimmed with white gauze, wild flowers and a black fringe cascading over the chignon.

Bonnets worn by widows and the elderly had very large and voluminous dark veils, but except for riding or travelling veils were not generally fashionable.

By the end of this period a more definite bonnet form with brimless back and wide ribbon ties had made its appearance.

Fig. 282 1862

Fig. 283 1870

Fig. 284 1872

Fig. 285 1872

Fig. 286 1876

Mid-Victorian

4 Hats 1860–1880

Although hats were not considered sufficiently respectable for church wear and very formal occasions they were gradually taking the place of bonnets, at least for younger women.

The low crowned hats with dipping brims and the pork pie hats were at first the main types, but soon a large variety of shapes was being worn. Among the most popular were styles with brims curving down at front and back and either curving up or turned up at the sides. The crowns tended to be either low and oval in shape or high and flat-topped. **Figs 287** and **288** illustrate examples of these hats, both of which were made of straw and had the veils which were usually worn for travelling or riding. Other fashionable styles of the 1860's were the *sailor*, with a rounded crown and a narrow straight brim, and a high crowned hat with a narrow brim.

The large masses of hair at the back of the head caused the hats to be worn well forward, but in the mid-'seventies they were perched on top and at the back of the head, though the tilted forward styles were still favoured.

In the early 1870's the high-crowned hats with brims turned up at one side or at the back were particularly fashionable and in fact high-crowned hats and toques were still being worn towards the end of the decade (**Figs 291** and **292**), and these developed into the most fashionable hats of the 'eighties.

The large brimmed hats in various styles were still popular for country and seaside wear. **Fig. 289** shows one example made of Tuscan straw and described as suitable for a "dressy toilette". Italian straw for expensive hats and Chinese rice straw for the cheaper end of the market was still the usual material for summer wear, together with horsehair plait. The latter was usually of Swiss manufacture for during the 1870's the English plaiting and straw hat manufacturing industry began to decline. Hats of black straw were worn for riding.

For winter wear felt began to be extensively used after having been out of fashion for many years. **Fig. 290** shows a version of the popular sailor hat made of this material. Trimming on hats, at first restricted to ribbon, gradually increased during the 1860's and became more and more profuse during the 1870's. Ribbons, especially of velvet, flowers and feathers were all used either alone or all together. Not only single feathers and small tufts, but wings and whole birds were a significant feature of the decoration of hats and bonnets towards the end of this period, and a sign of things to come. The bulk of feathers was imported from South America and the West Indies. In 1875 it was reported that a single consignment of 40,000 humming birds was common. A public outcry against the slaughter of birds for use in millinery was denounced as ridiculous by the *Milliner and Dressmaker*, "as the result of any ban on the use of feathers would simply be to deprive hundreds of respectable young women of their livelihood in the trade." In 1873 a "Lady" giving advice on how to dress on a limited budget remarked that feathers were a problem as good ostrich tips cost from four and sixpence to six shillings, but she suggested that if any of her readers kept poultry they might make a handsome aigrette with cock's feathers and the breast of a white fowl carefully skinned, rubbed with salt and pepper and dried in the sun or in the oven! The importance of suitable headwear for any woman who wished to appear a "lady" was shown by the fact that material for three bonnets and a hat with trimmings were together the second most expensive item in the yearly budget. The writer held that "nothing is more extravagant than parsimony in the matter of hats".

Fig. 287 1866

Fig. 289 1873

Fig. 288 1873

Fig. 290 1872

Fig. 291 1876

Fig. 292 1878

The Late Victorian Period
1880–1901

In the 1880's the fashionable woman was still extravagantly dressed and loaded with trimmings, her appearance reflecting the social and economic changes of the period. The rapid expansion of industry throughout the Victorian era had led to a considerable increase in prosperity for many. Mass production by machines and perfection of new techniques provided great quantities of cheap goods of every description, including a large variety of silk, wool, and "novelty" fabrics, lace and fancy trimmings.

In 1883 Paris reintroduced the bustle in a more exaggerated form, but this newest attempt to distort the female figure did not achieve much success in England where women were beginning to assert their independence and where the preference for more practical clothes was beginning to gain ground.

The long tight-fitting bodices of the late 'seventies buttoned up the front in jacket style had often been made separately from the skirts and this ensured a better fit for both parts and gave greater freedom of movement. This two-piece form of dress came into more general use during the 'eighties and eventually developed into the uniquely English *tailor-made* suit, a fashion which was to become universally popular, satisfying as it did the demand for simple clothes for an increasingly active life. In the meantime progress towards a more comfortable mode of dress was slow and a tightly corseted figure was still considered essential for elegance. The *wasp waist* was a feature of this period. The bodices of this decade were still of the jacket type, but with the return of the bustle they became shorter and frequently finished in a point at the front, emphasizing the tiny waist. Later the bodice was open down the front in a V-shape revealing a tucked, frilled or lace under-bodice. For day wear the neckline was very high, with a stand-up collar finished with lace edging or frills. There was little change in the sleeves, which remained close fitting to the elbow or mid forearm and ending in a cuff and frills. The bustle in its new shape, jutting out like a shelf, with an upward movement of the draperies from the back of the waist, was at the height of fashion about 1885, after which date its popularity declined slowly. In order to balance the great size of this bustle women were forced to adopt a curiously erect posture which seemed to be emphasized by the high hats and toques and the hair drawn up towards the top of the head.

Towards 1890 fashion interest moved away from the skirts and as their size subsided, the sleeves, the hats and to a lesser extent the bodices became the focus of attention. In the early 'nineties the main fullness in the skirt was still concentrated at the back and swept the floor behind, but in the course of the decade various gored and pleated styles were introduced curving over the hips and flaring out in a bell shape. The sleeves began to expand at the shoulder into the *leg-o'-mutton* style and by the mid 'nineties they had developed into huge puffs. At this time the silhouette of the fashionable woman resembled that of her counterpart of 70 years earlier. Once again this impracticable fashion soon disappeared and by the end of the century only small puffs remained at the tops of the sleeves.

Specific costumes were now being made for the different forms of sport in which women were taking part. These usually took the shape of a tailor made suit or *costume* consisting of a jacket and a ground-length skirt which might be ankle- or calf-length for cycling. A shirt blouse with a tie and a straw or felt *homburg* hat completed the outfit. The costume was also worn on other occasions and sometimes a frilly lace blouse was preferred instead of the masculine shirt.

In the last years of the century a special corset was designed to force women's figures into the S-shape which was to be fashionable throughout the Edwardian era. The blouse, as the separate bodice was now called, assumed great importance. It was gathered, pleated or tucked, trimmed with braid, frills or cascades of lace ruffles.

The neckline continued to be very high, supported by strips of whalebone. The tiny waist was accentuated by a sash or belt and the skirt still gored or pleated, spread widely round the feet. As the gowns were frequently very long, with trains sweeping the ground, it was necessary to lift the skirt when walking, thus revealing the ruffles of the petticoat. Taffeta was frequently used for petticoats or skirt linings and the rustling sound this produced as the wearer moved was considered very alluring. Colours were subdued or neutral, with white and pastel shades for evening wear, and soft lightweight fabrics such as lace, chiffon or velvet and supple wools were chosen to enhance the flowing curves of the figure and the graceful swing of the skirts.

The large, heavily trimmed hats of this era were among the most elaborate ever devised. At first they helped to balance the undulations of the fashionable shape, but when they reached maximum size in 1910–11 they gave a top-heavy, unbalanced appearance to the average figure, for by this date a fundamental change had at last occurred in women's fashions. Due to the influence of Paul Poiret, a brilliant Parisian designer, women were at last able to wear a simpler and comparatively comfortable style of dress. Corsets were less restricting, waistlines were higher and skirts were straight and slim. The *hobble* was an extreme form of the new narrow skirts and this style, together with the tunic overdress, loose kimono sleeves and feather-trimmed turban headwear was the result of Poiret's interest in the oriental costumes and settings designed by Léon Bakst for the Russian Ballet in 1909. Although these styles were often carried to extremes they were an indication of the revolution in dress which was to be given impetus by the events of the First World War.

Late Victorian

1 Hairstyles 1880–1901

Styles requiring large quantities of hair continued to be fashionable throughout the 1880's, the main mass being arranged in a large knot on the top or towards the back of the head and held in place with large ornamental hairpins or decorative combs. During the earlier years a fringe, either plain or consisting of small curls, was often worn low on the forehead (Figs 293, 294 and 295). This front hair was quite likely to be as false as the other curls, puffs and rolls which made up the fashionable coiffure. The general effect at this time was one of slight fluffiness, with soft waves at the sides of the head. The latest "coiffure novelty" invented by Mr. J. Lichtenfeld, Coiffeur Français, of Oxford Street consisted of "a set of combs with an attachment of large and full, or of snow curls. The insertion of these combs gives all the effect of elaborate dressing of the natural hair, whether in the form of a coronet to fill up the spaces of plaits or twists, or as appendages to any part of the head. . . . The twists or strands made by this artist have no cumbrous frizettes inside. They are all made of long hair, the inner part of which is slightly crimped so as to impart at the same time both fullness and lightness. Six of the pieces in which they are made up suffice to form any fashionable headdress. His separate rococo curls are also a novelty well calculated to fill up."

It was early in this period that Marcel Grateau achieved success with his special technique for giving the hair a natural-looking wave. Discovered almost by accident this wave was called *ondulations* or the *moiré* or *watered* effect, but much later it took the name of its creator. At the end of 1884 Marcel had many celebrated clients and his invention was the beginning of a new era in hairdressing.

The appearance of the hair in the 'nineties was one of fullness and softness, with the sides still drawn up off the ears. False hair pieces were not used so much as they had been, but women made the most of their natural hair by fluffing, frizzing or curling. Towards the middle of the decade the top knot became extremely fashionable (Fig. 297 and Fig. 298). It was arranged in a variety of styles and positions, but was usually twisted into a round "bun" on top of the head. Occasionally it was placed well forward and blended with the front puff, fringe or loose waves, or it might be a coil in the nape of the neck. In the mid 'nineties it projected from the back of the head in a twisted knob known popularly as the "door knocker" style. Frames were used to increase the size of the bun. It was fashionable to part the hair in the centre or slightly to one side, but soft curls or a fluffy fringe over the forehead continued to be popular throughout this period, probably because many of the hats and bonnets were of a style for which forehead curls seemed appropriate. For evening wear ornaments were worn, such as feathery aigrettes, ribbon bows and elaborate combs and pins of jet, shell and amber decorated with jewels and cut steel or enamelled designs.

Dyeing of the hair continued, although women were constantly being warned against its hazards.

Fig. 293 1883

Fig. 294 1890

Fig. 295 1885

Fig. 296 1893

Fig. 297 1899

Fig. 298 1898

Late Victorian

2 Hats 1880–1901

During the first few years of this period there was little noticeable change in the general style of hats and bonnets and the manner in which they were worn, that is, either tilted forward or more usually towards the back of the head. In 1884, however, a new style of hat appeared which was to remain fashionable for several years and was especially characteristic of the 1880's. The crown of this hat was shaped like an inverted flower pot and was usually very high, although lower forms did occur. As a rule the brim was narrow and was turned up at the back as shown in **Fig. 299**, although it might also be turned up at one side and sometimes at both sides. A variation of this style, with a lower crown and the brim widening and projecting out at the front, occurred in 1888. The crowns of toques and bonnets also grew higher and the brims often formed a pointed arch in front. Feathers and trimmings were all designed to add to the height (**Fig. 300**). Even when the crowns became somewhat lower in the late 'eighties the illusion of height was still preserved by means of stiffened bows or, more especially, of feathers. A pointed or arched effect was often given to quite small hats by means of pairs of wings or complete birds placed in a position of swooping flight (**Fig. 302**). There was little discernible difference between bonnets, or capotes as they were still often called, and toques. The former had ribbon ties fixed well to the back which were discarded during the late 1880's, but they reappeared in narrower form about 1890. The bonnets had become extremely small by this time and often could not be seen for trimming. They tended more and more to be worn only by older women, the toque being fashionable for the young as also were the crownless wreath-shaped bonnets which came into fashion in the late 'eighties.

In addition to felt and velvet, beaver and plush were fabrics much used for winter wear. Straw was popular for winter as well as summer hats and was frequently combined with velvet which was used either as trimming or as lining for the brim and sometimes in alternating rows with the straw plait to make the actual fabric. Braid was also used in this manner. Coarse straw plaits and open-work plaits were also much used, but the latter were less delicate than those which had been used in the early Victorian period.

Throughout the 1890's the shapes and sizes of hats varied tremendously and it is difficult to trace any particular line of development. Toques with high crowns continued and **Fig. 303** shows one with the fashionable drum-shaped or hour-glass crown. It was made of green velvet and the elaborate trimming so typical of this period consisted of a scarf of cream-coloured *point d'esprit* (lace) knotted in the centre under a large cabochon of pearl and crystal with black osprey feathers and a white upstanding aigrette. This fashion for high ornaments of feathers or wired lace or ribbon continued throughout the period. Hats were still worn straight on top of the head. There were many variations of the large-brimmed type. **Fig. 304** shows a style with a projecting front brim. Some brims were flat and straight, some were turned up in front or curved up each side. Others curved down from left to right (**Fig. 301**). In addition to straw, velvet and felt, a number of light materials such as lace and chiffon were used for summer wear and flowers were heaped on in great quantities. The vogue for large hats required the use of long pins with ornamental heads in a great variety of designs (see page 143).

Fig. 299 1884

Fig. 300 1886

Fig. 301 1897

Fig. 302 1888

Fig. 303 1896

Fig. 304 1893

Late Victorian

3   Hats   1880–1901

Hats of the "sailor" type became extremely popular during the late 1880's, not only for summer sports such as tennis or sailing but also for general wear with the plainer dresses or costumes. There were many variations in the height of crown and width of brim. During the late 'eighties and early 'nineties a style with the brim wider in front was fashionable. They were, of course, made of straw and were always plainly trimmed with a ribbon band and occasionally a bow or loops. **Fig. 306** shows a sailor hat with a fairly high crown and wide brim. A narrower brim was fashionable the following year.

The increasing feminine participation in sport during this period necessitated the designing of appropriate clothes and headwear for various activities. Although the sailor hat was usually worn for tennis other less suitable styles were also adopted **(Fig. 305)**. For walking or cycling a felt homburg hat with the brim turned up at each side was considered appropriate. This style, with a high crown cleft like a man's trilby, appeared in the 'nineties **(Fig. 307)**. More elaborate hats were permissible for skating and **Fig. 309** illustrates an example made of coarse straw trimmed with silk ribbon and quills. The upturned, silk-lined brim shows the bead embroidery which was common during this period. This illustration also shows the fashionable "door knocker" hairstyle.

There were many hats which were designed for wear with bathing costume. Although generally made of oiled silk or a similar proofed fabric most of them resembled the fashionable styles of the time and must have been useless for keeping the hair dry.

Trimmings of feathers and birds reached extraordinary proportions and were quite usual even for sports and riding hats. The variety of these feathered ornaments and the destruction of bird life which was entailed in order to maintain this flourishing industry may be judged from some of the descriptions in *The Millinery Record* in 1896. Capercalzie quills or fancy mounts of impeyan wings with crested pigeon aigrettes were used for cycling hats. Amazon parrot wings mounted in sets of four "look well outspread on a network of tulle on large hats". Cock's feathers and quills were common and the wings of magpies and sometimes the whole bird were considered elegant. Another typical decoration was a pair of wings of cream-coloured horsehair shaped like pigeon's wings and studded with humming birds' breast feathers. The hat ornament in **Fig. 308** which was very typical consisted of an aigrette of bird-of-paradise feathers springing from a tuft of white feathers and tiny white Java sparrows. Osprey feathers, which had been most popular were beginning to be replaced by ostrich plumes, always a favourite ornament and destined to become more so during the Edwardian era which followed.

Veils of net, tulle or gauze frequently patterned with spots and in a colour to match the hat or costume became very popular during this period. Short veils reaching the tip of the nose were worn over smaller hats and under large ones during the early 'eighties. By 1890 larger veils were becoming fashionable. These covered the face entirely and were pulled in under the chin by a string or were pinned at the back of the neck **(Fig. 310)**. Very long veils about three yards in length were crossed behind the head and brought round to be tied in front across the throat. Veils were also used to secure all types of hats during sporting activities, especially cycling and motoring. The vogue for veiled hats continued into the next period.

Fig. 305 1888

Fig. 306 1887

Fig. 307 1895

Fig. 308

Fig. 309 1896

Fig. 310 1900

Edwardian

4 Hairstyles 1901–1914

Hairstyles of this period were characterized by an appearance of very soft fullness. To be fashionable a mass of thick wavy hair was essential. Those who were not lucky enough to be naturally endowed with this important asset made use of frames, pads and false hair, and even those who had plenty of their own frequently added an extra length in order to give the necessary fullness, especially to the *pompadour* style. This was similar to **Fig. 312** and it continued to be popular for the first few years of the Edwardian period. For this coiffure the use of pads combined with French combing, i.e. "back combing", was usually necessary. The back hair was brushed up from the nape of the neck and arranged in a rather flat coil or plait on the crown of the head. *Low styles*, as they were called, were also popular, the back hair being arranged in a vertical coil or plait lying fairly low on the neck **(Fig. 311)**. Whatever style was chosen a considerable degree of width was considered essential, with the ears always revealed and the forehead almost completely hidden by small curls or large soft waves or bands of hair. The *transformation* made of natural wavy hair was introduced in 1902. This aid to hairdressing could be adapted to any of the fashionable styles.

The first permanent waving process was finally perfected in 1904 by Karl Nessler, a German hairdresser who established himself in New York under the name of "Nestlé". The first "perms" took up to 12 hours to complete and were extremely expensive. The majority of women had to achieve the all-important waves and curls by means of curling tongs and the other curling devices on the market. All kinds of fancy combs and special "hair-ties" were also available for securing the carefully-arranged tresses, whether real or artificial.

In 1908 the hair tended to become even wider on either side of the head in order to support the wide crowned hats which became fashionable that year **(Fig. 313)**.

Around 1911 the fashionable hair styles began to conform more closely to the shape of the head. The width above the ears which had been necessary to balance the enormous hats was now reduced and the hair was drawn loosely back to cover or partially cover the ears. Whilst the hair was still often arranged in a coil or knot on top of the head the fashionable trend was to have the bulk of the hair towards the back of the head in Grecian style. In 1913–14 coiffures were still in a state of transition, and when the hair was not piled on the crown of the head in waves or smooth coils it was puffed out, sometimes with the aid of a transformation, half-way between the nape of the neck and the crown of the head **(Fig. 316)**, whilst for evening wear the required height was gained by plumes wired to stand erect or sometimes at an oblique angle **(Fig. 314)**. Bandeaux made of light material embroidered with silver, or of spangled or beaded net were sometimes worn for evening. These were swathed round the head in imitation of the turban head-dresses which had been designed by Paul Poiret in Paris in 1911. Thin jewelled bands were also worn, as well as other ornaments such as jewelled matching sets consisting of a comb or *barette* (an ornament sometimes set on a comb) and two hairpins. Some hairpins which were available had ornamental ends set on a pivot so that they could be bent to the shape of the head **(Fig. 317)**. Ordinary hair pins for securing the hair were, of course, similar to modern ones, although much larger and made of heavier gauge wire.

Fig. 311 1905

Fig. 312 1906

Fig. 313 1908

Fig. 314 1913

Fig. 315 1911

Fig. 316 1914

Fig. 317 1913

Edwardian

5 Hats 1901–1911

The hats of this period were always large and very elaborately trimmed, especially for summer wear when flowers, lace, tulle, chenille and feathers might all form the decoration of one straw hat. Felt winter hats were somewhat plainer, with low crowns, but these might be covered with loops or ruchings of ribbon with quills and jewelled ornaments. Trimmings and materials were frequently combined in an extravagant manner, for instance a fur toque with camellias or a fur hat with a cache-peigne of old rose velvet and silk roses and an ornament of upstanding plumes and ostrich feather tufts. Ostrich plumes were especially popular during this period. At first hats were worn uncompromisingly straight on top of the head, but by 1904 they were set at all angles. An extreme forward tilt was very fashionable and in many cases this was so exaggerated that a cache-peigne of flowers or ruched material was necessary to cover the space between the underside of the back brim and the back of the head (**Fig. 321**). Many hats and toques, although worn straight, had the back brims narrow or turned up and wider in front, projecting well forward. An extraordinary variety of materials was used, including paper, a fabric by no means new in the history of hats as it was certainly used in the eighteenth century. *Tagel* was another popular material. This was formed of tiny plaits of hemp strands.

In 1908 the most fashionable hats had large wide crowns almost entirely covered with flowers, and they were once more worn straight (**Fig. 322**). The following year the crowns became lower but remained very wide, and the brims also increased in circumference and continued to do so until 1911. These large hats were not suitable for sportswear, so smaller styles were introduced. **Fig. 323** shows an example suggested for golf or fishing but the straw sailor or "boater" of the 1880's was still a great favourite for all occasions and was, of course, always worn straight on top of the head.

For those who preferred to wear their large hats when taking part in the new sport of motoring, an all-enveloping veil was a necessity to protect the hair from dust and to help keep the hat on securely. The example illustrated in **Fig. 324** was waterproof and had a self-gripping adjuster. Apart from large hat pins, bandeaux were devised to keep the hats firmly and comfortably in position. These took the form of circular, saucer-shaped fitments made in stiffened material with an opening for the head. They were fitted inside the hats, filling the space between the large crown and the wearer's head.

Fig. 318 shows two types of hatpin used during this period.

Fig. 318

Fig. 319 1902

Fig. 320 1905

Fig. 321 1906

Fig. 322 1908

Fig. 323 1906

Fig. 324 1911

Edwardian

6 Hats 1911–1914

The enormous hats of the late Edwardian period reached their maximum width in 1911 (**Fig. 325** and **Fig. 326**). They were secured to the elaborate coiffures by long hat pins, with large decorative heads made of jet, leather, enamel and carved ivory in the shape of flowers or huge coloured stones such as amethyst or topaz in settings of gold or cut steel (**Fig. 318** on previous page). The projecting points were such a potential danger in crowded places that protective butts were invented which could be put over the points once the pins were in position.

Tall crowned hats had been designed during the preceding years, but these met with little success until 1911–12, when the wide brimmed hats, having reached in extreme cases a circumference of two yards, were finally beginning to be abandoned. The high hats had vertical trimmings of large ribbon loops and twists or arrangements of flowers wired to stand erect, and plumes were as popular as ever (**Fig. 327**). High trimmings also appeared on the wide-brimmed hats. Conical and square-shaped crowns were also in evidence.

In 1912 styles became smaller, with large crowns fitting lower on the head and small or medium brims. Feathers were set upright, either at one side or at back or front of the hat. Sometimes they were set at an angle, or two might be set at opposite angles to one another. Brims were often designed to give an effect of flight even when no trimmings were added.

Fig. 325 1910

Fig. 326 1911

Fig. 327 1911

Fig. 328 1911–1912

Fig. 329 1912

Fig. 330 1913

The First World War, involving almost the whole of the civilized world and bringing about the death of millions of men, affected profoundly the way of life of people of every class. Women's dress, as always, continued to reflect not only the shift of social and economic forces dominating society, but also the change in their own status which was speeded by the events of the war years and confirmed by the right to vote obtained in 1918 by those over 30. Perhaps there was some significance in the fact that within a few years women began to adopt those symbols of freedom, the short skirt and short hair: and it was not until 1928 when the younger women or *flappers* became enfranchised that more feminine fashions returned to favour.

It was not until 1915 that any alteration in fashion became apparent. The popular tunic overskirt tended to be longer whilst the underskirt remained at ankle length and was still quite narrow. Shortage of material and the growing involvement of women in war work of all kinds increased the demand for plain, practical clothing, and in 1916 rather full, flared skirts appeared with hems just below calf length, thus giving freedom of leg movement. Long, loose-fitting, high-collared coats were worn, as well as short jackets and three-quarter length or waist-length coats and capes. Tailored suits were particularly popular and were adopted by those doing men's work for which a uniform was usual. Plain, dark colours were now used in contrast to the bright, strong hues associated with Poiret's pre-war designs. Skirts became straighter towards the end of the war and remained more or less at the same length until 1922, when for a year or so the hemline returned to the ankles, but after this they became steadily shorter until for the first time in the history of clothes women's legs were revealed up to the knee.

The waistline had been around or slightly above the natural level between 1910 and 1922, and had been emphasized by a belt or sash. Now, a flat boyish figure was the ideal, dresses became straight with an unbroken line from shoulder to hem, the bodice joining the skirt low on the hips. Hip-length knitted jumpers, a recent invention, and long blouses worn over the skirt added to the tubular effect of the silhouette, as did the straight-cut jackets of the tailored suits. The apparent denial of femininity in the fashions of the 'twenties, the beginning of the new age of freedom, was carried to further extremes when women cut off their long hair and hid what remained of it beneath the plainest and most unbecoming hats ever designed. By 1927, when skirts were at their shortest and hair was Eton-cropped, women's figures had acquired a squareness of outline which was repeated in the high cloche hats of that year. The limit of the fashion seemed to have been reached and the inevitable reaction was becoming evident in 1929 when hemlines began to dip once again. Perhaps women had become used to their emancipated status and more feminine styles were now acceptable. At all events by 1931 hemlines had reached below calf length and the fashionable look was one of extreme length and slenderness. Skirts were cut on the cross or had inset gores or panels to ensure a clinging fit over the hips with movement below the knees. The waistline returned to its natural position and belts and sashes were usual accessories. Wrap-over coats were shaped in a similar way to dresses and large fur collars framed heads wearing tiny hats tilted to show as much "permed" hair as possible. Backless evening dresses with floor-length hemlines were now generally fashionable. By the mid 'thirties skirts for day-wear were around 12 or 13 inches from the ground and still slim with gores or inverted pleats. Tailored suits had long jackets with broad lapels and single or treble button fastening.

Since the 'twenties it had become customary for young women to go about hatless on informal occasions, but hats were always worn outdoors by the majority of women. An infinite variety of styles was available during the 'thirties.

From 1937 skirts became steadily shorter and clothes and hats increasingly fussy and decorative. Shoulders were widened by means of gathered puff sleeves on dresses and padding in coats and jackets. Sleeves were usually inset, but the raglan style was also used for coats. Three-quarter unbelted "swagger" coats were worn, as well as fitted styles with belts. A great range of fabrics of every kind was in use, all in a variety of weaves and textures. The favourite hat materials were still felt and straw.

Throughout the Second World War the rationing of new clothes and material by means of an allowance of coupons, a number of which had, in England, to be given up whenever garments were purchased, led to a boom in the second-hand clothing trade and a "freezing" of fashion for almost eight years. The skirt length remained just below the knee and shoulders were padded to give a very square appearance. Sweaters and skirts became the popular everyday wear for most women and much hand knitting was done with whatever wool was available.

The famous "New Look" introduced by the Paris designer Christian Dior began to affect the London fashion scene in 1947, and by the following year most Englishwomen had managed to buy or make themselves one or two garments in the new and graceful fashion. Long sweeping skirts flaring from a fitted waist line gave a feeling of femininity and luxuriousness long missing from women's clothes. Shoulders were softly rounded and suit jackets short and closely fitted with flared basques. There was a renewed interest in hats, which were usually off-the-face and decorated with feathers. Clothes rationing came to an end in England in 1949 and materials could then be bought in greater quantity and variety. The new nylon fabric was in great demand.

The early 'fifties saw the continuation of the more feminine style of dress. The small-waisted look was still popular in dresses and suits, but skirts for day wear tended to become narrower, with some fullness below the hips in the form of pleats or gores. Permanent pleating was now possible and all-round knife-pleated skirts were popular. Very full skirts were usual for summer dresses and the short evening gowns which came into fashion in this decade. Stiffened underskirts and frilly petticoats were worn with many of these *bouffant* styles. Full-length evening dresses were considered correct for balls and grand occasions. Strapless tops were fashionable for evening and beach wear, the bodice being boned to conform to the figure. Loose-fitting coats were either hip-length or full-length, with dolman or raglan sleeves and large collars. A straight wrap-around style, with loose fitting sleeves and shawl collar, was also popular. Skirt lengths remained about mid calf until after the middle of the decade, when the hemline began to rise once again. By 1960 skirts were slim, usually with a pleat at the back to allow for easier walking. Tops were inclined to be easy fitting, with collars standing away from the neck. Jackets and coats were straight and loose fitting, shoulders on all garments being rounded. The high hair styles and hats tended to balance the straight narrow skirts and to offset the slight bulkiness of the upper part of the fashionable figure.

The simplicity of line and cut which is the keynote of modern fashion was well established by this date, and fashionable clothes might be found to suit most types of figure and all age groups.

Twentieth Century

1 1914–1918

During the First World War there was little change in hair styles and hat fashions. The hair, dressed low on the forehead and partially covering the ears, was drawn back into a bun or coil. A few women, busy with war work and finding long hair impracticable and also perhaps revelling in a spirit of emancipation cut off their hair to a level just below the ears, but the "bob" was not generally adopted until after the war. Women working in munition factories and other types of work where the hair needed protection from machinery and dirt frequently wore a kind of mob cap similar in style to the bathing caps of the period (**Fig. 334**).

High-crowned toques (**Fig. 333**) and hats with large round crowns and wide brims similar to those in vogue in the late Edwardian era continued to be worn throughout the war years, and also another, wide-brimmed type with a shallow flat crown (**Fig. 331**). Some hats were worn with a sideways tilt (**Fig. 332**). Except for dressy occasions a plain band or a rosette of ribbon was the most usual form of trimming.

Women doing men's jobs as bus or tram crews, postwomen, policewomen or farm workers in the Women's Land Army, where an official uniform was normally worn, wore either a peaked cap similar to those of the men or hats of straw or felt with dome-shaped crowns and fairly wide brims. These were trimmed with a plain ribbon band and the appropriate badge. The example shown in **Fig. 337** is a hat of this type worn by a woman delivering milk. This style was also adopted by all ranks of the Women's Army Auxiliary Corps which was formed in the Spring of 1917 (**Fig. 336**). Officers of the Women's Royal Naval Service, which was formed in November of the same year, wore a large *tricorne* hats (**Fig. 338**), whilst ratings wore the kind of hat with a pleated crown shown in **Fig. 339**. This style, with modifications, probably formed the basis of the cap which was designed for the Women's Royal Air Force when it was first established in April 1918, and which, with more up-to-date shaping, was worn by the W.R.A.F. and W.A.T.S. (formerly W.A.A.C.) in the Second World War (see page 157).

Fig. 331 1917

Fig. 333 1916

Fig. 332 1916

Fig. 335 1917

Fig. 334 1917

Fig. 336 1918

Fig. 337 1917

Fig. 338 1918

Fig. 339 1918

Twentieth Century

2 Hairstyles 1918–1930

For several years after the end of the war most women continued to wear their hair drawn back close to the head, with a loose coil or bun projecting at the back or occasionally placed fairly high in the Grecian style of the pre-war era. Large "Spanish" combs, jewelled, carved or plain in many varieties of tortoiseshell were worn by the fashionable at the back or to one side of the coiffure. These combs served no special purpose; they were merely decorative and were put in anywhere **(Fig. 340)**.

Bobbed hair was gradually being adopted by the majority, much to the dismay of hairdressers who each year hopefully predicted the end of the craze. Introduced during the war years it was at first a medium short, straight cut the whole way round the head, the ends being "clubbed" almost level **(Fig. 341)**. The total length was usually level with the bottom tips of the ears. Later many variations were evolved as methods of cutting became more skilled.

Switches of hair were imported, mostly from Italy, and the "postiche" was created for those who regretted cutting off their hair, in order, according to a hairdressing Journal, to "transform out of date and unsightly bobbed hair into a becoming and artistic coiffure". But in spite of all predictions the bob became increasingly popular and by 1924 was in full fashion. Even shorter hair in the *shingle* style appeared in 1923 and soon rivalled the bob. Developed in France by a Parisian hairdresser, it was a method of cutting the hair by means of tapering which, in the hands of a skilled operator, could be adapted to suit any shape of head. The early form of shingle was short and exposed the hair line at the back of the neck. By 1925 it was fairly common, the hair being cut to follow the shape of the head with perhaps a slight fringe and soft waves at the sides **(Figs 342 and 343)**.

Those who preferred to keep their hair long wore it drawn closely and smoothly to the head; the back ends were rolled into neat curls turned under or braided to look as short as possible. The plait of hair might be artificial and kept in position by a narrow headband **(Fig. 345)**. Coiled "earphones" were also popular and, according to a fashion magazine, this fashion was often adopted by serious-minded women! Bandeaux of every description were fashionable, especially for evening wear, including narrow ones of diamanté or broad ones of beadwork, silver lace or silver thread embroidery **(Fig. 344)**. Some, known as *shingle bands*, were artfully designed to cover the shorn back of the head.

In 1926 there appeared the extremely short boyish style known as the *Eton crop*, the hair being straight and cut well above the ears **(Fig. 346)**. Later this was modified by longer side pieces curled forward on to the cheeks.

In 1929 the shingle began to be worn a little longer **(Fig. 347)** and the back hair was often long enough to be formed into a small roll or bun. By 1930 the hair was becoming longer at the sides, with roll curls or small flat pin curls at the nape of the neck.

Fig. 340 1920

Fig. 341 1922

Fig. 342 1925

Fig. 343 1924

Fig. 344 1923

Fig. 345 1924

Fig. 346 1926

Fig. 347 1929

Twentieth Century

3 Hats 1918–1930

Large crowned hats with wide brims continued to be popular after the War and they remained in vogue until the early 'twenties. They were worn straight and came well down over the brow, whilst the brims dipped on either side or were slightly tilted usually to the right. In 1921 it was fashionable to have the trimmings projecting over the brim **(Fig. 348)** There was a good deal of controversy over the use of plumage in millinery and two Bills were put forward by a number of M.P.s, one to prohibit the importation of the plumage of birds and the second to prohibit the sale or possession of plumage illegally imported. Apart from feathers and flowers or fruit such as hanging bunches of cherries, trimming included embroidery, particularly over the crown and upper side of the brim. **Fig. 349** shows a black velvet toque embroidered in silver. An enormous variety of materials were used for hats and beautiful handwork was a characteristic of the more expensive millinery, for example flowers made of hand-painted tape, with leaves of leather, were sewn all over a white silk hat, whilst embroidered and painted kid toques were recommended for travelling or motoring.

As short hair became more general small close-fitting hats were obviously appropriate, and in 1923 the *cloche* appeared. These hats, with their deep crowns and narrow brims, were pulled down to the eyes, obscuring half the wearer's face and all her hair with the exception of a curl or two on either cheek. Trimmings, flat and rather restrained, consisted usually of ribbon or material in contrasting colours. **Fig. 353** shows trimmings of leather.

By 1926 the cloche was universally worn. It became very deep in the crown and was either brimless or had a small brim which was sometimes turned up at the front or at one side **(Figs 350, 351 and 352)**. In 1928 hats with drooping sides and uneven brims were shown in Paris, and also brims that were lengthened on one side only or were rather long at the back in a style reminis-

cent of a Sou'wester. In the following year crowns were becoming shallower, although they were still plain, and brims were getting larger. They were sometimes draped and folded flat against the crown **(Fig. 355)**. Eyes and eyebrows were beginning to reappear, flowers were once more being used for trimming, and a softer more dressy look was apparent by 1930. **Fig. 354** shows the type of hat which was popular for summer wear at the end of the decade. The beret, which had made a first appearance in the 'twenties, was one of many styles which were to gain popularity in the coming years (see **Fig. 365** on page 157).

Fig. 348 1921

Fig. 349 1921

Fig. 350 1926

Fig. 351 1924

Fig. 352 1928

Fig. 354 1930

Fig. 353 1927

Fig. 355 1929

Twentieth Century

4 Hairstyles 1930–1939

Throughout the early part of the 'thirties the bob and modified forms of the shingle were worn by almost all women. Methods of tapering the hair shorter at the top and leaving it longer at the neck to allow the formation of curls led to the creation of styles known as the *Cringle* **(Fig. 357)** and the *Mingle*. Close deep waves and little flat pin curls were now a feature of hairdressing as regular visits to the hairdresser for ''perms'' and ''sets'' became a routine for many women. Water waving and a modern form of Marcel waving were also much used.

With improved methods of permanent waving and increasing skill in cutting and tapering, hairdressers were able to create many different styles for short hair. One which was adopted by many fashionable women in 1932 was the *Wind-blown* or *Windswept* coiffure followed by the *Will-of-the-Wisp* in 1933 **(Fig. 360)**. Famous film stars provided fashions for their many admirers to follow. The long bob worn by Greta Garbo and the ''platinum blonde'' hair of Jean Harlow were examples of this kind. By 1935 curls of all sorts were being worn, crest and roll curls, *coxcomb* curls across the side of the head and partial fringes **(Figs 358 and 359)**. One style consisted of a wreath of curls all round the head with a smooth crown and a special cap was designed to go with it.

In 1937 an upward and off-the-face tendency in styling was apparent and perhaps owed something to the coiffures created for peeresses to wear with their coronets at the Coronation that year. Hair was now being worn much longer and the development of the ''ends perm'' made it possible to have a smooth effect with curled ends. In 1937 and 1938 two trends were noticeable, the long, often shoulder-length *page boy* style, usually fairly straight with the ends curled under, and the upswept or *Edwardian* coiffure **(Figs 363 and 364)**. For the latter, the long back hair was brushed up and over the back of the head, the ends forming a mass of curls on top and towards the front. In both styles the hair was usually swept up from the temples and ears in roll curls.

The page-boy style with variations was easy to care for and, to the dismay of hairdressers, it became extremely popular with younger women and remained so for nearly a decade.

Fig. 356   1931

Fig. 357   1932

Fig. 358   1934

Fig. 359   1934

Fig. 360   1933

Fig. 361   1937

Fig. 362   1938

Fig. 363   1937

Fig. 364   1938/39

Twentieth Century

5 Hats 1930–1939

During the early years of this decade hats became very small, with narrow brims or none at all, and were perched on the side of the head at an acute angle (**Figs 365, 366** and **367**). Short "eye" veils were a popular innovation. Pill box styles, berets and knitted hats of all kinds were fashionable.

In 1934 the *Tyrolean* style was introduced and remained popular for a number of years. *Cossack* hats of fur or astrakan, *fez* and tricorne shapes were also worn. Although many hats still had a sideways tilt others were now being worn towards the back of the head, but in the summer of 1935 hats with low crowns and wide brims were still tilted to the right (**Fig. 368**). The *Juliet* cap appeared in this year. This was a small round skull cap intended to be worn with the hair in a halo of curls. Made in white beads or pearls it was also a popular bridal headdress.

In 1936 height was becoming important either in the crown or the trimming. The Tyrolean or *Robin Hood* hats made in felt or suede, with the crowns shaped to a point with tucks or folds, were set at various angles and decorated with pheasant tail feathers or similar long quills (**Fig. 369**). A similar style without a brim, and draped turbans, cossack and fez styles were popular, together with numerous other shapes such as *sombreros, pill boxes* and toques worn at different angles. Throughout the last years of the 'thirties hats became more and more varied, and although in 1938 many were still worn towards the back of the head, or at a sideways angle, including the felt Tyrolean type which was still in evidence and the *Breton* sailor with upturned brim (**Fig. 372**), a pronounced forward tilt was becoming fashionable. Large berets, toques decorated with flowers, draped turbans and triangular kerchiefs (for holiday wear) were styles seen during the last two years of the decade.

Caps swathed in chiffon in several colours and turbans of jersey fabric with scarves attached were among the styles of the winter of 1938–39, but the most popular hats of these two years were those perched forward. Most, if not all, of these had either a band of matching material round the back of the head to keep them in position or a piece of thin elastic, either black or brown, which was drawn under the back hair. Eye veils and swathes of net veiling were popular trimmings (**Figs 370** and **371**).

Fig. 366 1932

Fig. 367 1931

Fig. 365 1930

Fig. 368 1935

Fig. 370 1939

Fig. 369 1936

Fig. 371 1939

Fig. 372 1938

Twentieth Century

6 Headwear 1939–1945

The hairstyles which had been evolved during the later years of the 'thirties were adapted to war-time requirements and worn throughout the war years, changing little until the end of the 'forties. Women in the Services, and in other jobs in which the wearing of a uniform of some kind was required naturally adopted a short style which was easy to look after and which looked neat and appropriate with a military style cap or hat. The *Liberty* cut was designed to meet the need for an attractive and practical "hair-do" and one of several versions of this cut is shown in **Fig. 374**. The hair was cut short and waved diagonally across the back of the head, ending in flat neat curls with a few flattened roll curls at the sides and top. For those who preferred to have their hair longer the horseshoe roll curving around the back of the head was neat and easy to care for, and the page-boy style continued to be popular. The front hair was swept up into curls or waves or turned under to form horns. Bleaching was more fashionable than ever and many women treated their hair at home with preparations containing peroxide.

These war years marked the beginning of the decline in hat wearing. Although some hats were available in the shops and were not "on coupons", as were all other articles of clothing, women discovered that hats were no longer a necessity. Those they already possessed were worn for special occasions, but no new styles appeared. When a head covering was needed a long scarf or piece of material was wound round the head and knotted on top to form a turban, or a large square could be arranged in similar fashion **(Fig. 373)**. The head square worn peasant-fashion **(Fig. 375)** was also generally adopted and continued to be popular with women in all walks of life for many years.

Women in the W.R.A.F. wore caps similar in design to those worn by their predecessors in 1918. These were of the same grey-blue cloth as the uniforms with hard shiny peaks **(Fig. 376)**. The chief difference between the caps of officers and those of the ranks was the more elaborate badge on the former consisting of a crown and wings. All ranks in the A.T.S. wore forage caps with metal badges **(Fig. 377)** or caps similar to those of the W.R.A.F. with fabric peaks **(Fig. 379)**. W.R.N.S. ratings wore round caps with ribbon trim similar to those worn by the men **(Fig. 378)**. The black felt tricornes of the officers were trimmed with stitched bands, the badges being mainly of gilt metal thread **(Fig. 380)**.

Fig. 373 1940

Fig. 374 1942

Fig. 375 1941

Fig. 376 1944

Fig. 377 1942

Fig. 378 1944

Fig. 379 1942

Fig. 380 1944

Twentieth Century

7 Hair and hats 1945–1950

For two years after the end of the War women's hair fashions followed those of the previous decade. Among the young very long hair was still favoured, either with or without curls or rolls over the forehead (**Fig. 381**). The back hair was sometimes pinned back in a roll or cluster of curls (**Fig. 382**). The *Bubble* cut, in which the hair was cut very short all over the head and formed into small curls, was a fashion tried out by the more adventurous in 1946 but it was not until Christian Dior introduced the New Look in clothes that a real change in hairdressing styles became apparent. A new look in shorter hair was produced by hairdressers, and the *gamine* or *urchin* cut was introduced, see page 162 (**Fig. 392**). For a year or two, however, most women preferred to keep their hair fairly long, the most popular length being from two to three inches at the nape of the neck, ears and temple and six inches at the crown. An upswept style was also in vogue (**Fig. 383**).

In 1945 and 1946 hats, when worn, were still fairly flat and tilted forward (**Fig. 384**), but in the winter of 1946 small hats were designed to be worn towards the back of the head, many of them draped with scarves attached to the side, back or crown (**Fig. 387**), a look appropriate to the severe weather of the early months of 1947. During that year hats began to come into their own once more. Off-the-face styles were firmly established, often with a pronounced side slant (**Figs 385** and **386**). Most hats had trimming placed to one side and often drooping downwards. Large bunches of feathers or one or two long plumes were very popular decorations and continued to be so for several years.

Fig. 381 1946

Fig. 383 1949

Fig. 382 1946

Fig. 384 1946

Fig. 385 1947

Fig. 386 1950

Fig. 387 1947

Twentieth Century

8 Hair 1950–1960

Short hair was highly fashionable during the early years of the 'fifties, although most women preferred to have their hair medium length at the back. For evening wear especially, hair dressed on the neck was more flattering with off-the-shoulder gowns than upswept or shingled styles. Earrings were a popular form of jewellery during this time.

Soap ceased to be rationed in September 1950, but increasing use was made of the "soapless" shampoos which had been first introduced in the 'thirties, and throughout this decade all kinds of shampoos for every type of hair came on the market, as well as tints and dyes, lacquers, setting lotions and preparations of every description designed to improve the condition and appearance of the hair. Home permanent waving kits were available for those who were too busy or who could not afford the regular visits to a hairdresser which many women now regarded as a necessity. The standard of craftsmanship in good salons was steadily rising. A softer and more natural appearance could now be given to the hair by cold waving and tepid waving methods, and improved skill in cutting enabled women to have casual, natural-looking hair styles.

In 1956 a trend towards longer hair was being encouraged by hairdressers who introduced the *bouffant* styles. This arrangement of the hair was achieved by the use of large rollers for setting and then by back-combing to give height and fullness, and afterwards lightly brushing the hair across the top to give a smooth effect. By 1959 this smoother, less curly, look was fashionable. Hair was short and swirling or bouffant, with the forehead covered partially or completely. Longer hair was swept up, back brushed and swathed into a dome or *bee-hive* shape (**Fig. 395**), the ends being folded vertically at the back into a French pleat. Young girls favoured the *pony-tail* which was introduced at this time. The hair was brushed smoothly from the forehead and up from the nape of the neck to be fastened high on the crown with a ribbon or specially-designed circular clasp and the ends allowed to swing freely in a "tail".

In 1960 many styles were to be seen. The majority of women preferred to wear their hair short, but with the aid of skilful cutting, shaping and waving and a wide variety of preparations everyone could have healthy attractive hair arranged in the style of their choice.

A revival of the form of bandeau known popularly as the "Alice band" occurred during the later years of this decade and continued into the 'sixties. Examples could be bought ready made in a variety of materials including velvet, tortoiseshell, and coloured plastic. The style was based on the ribbon which tied back the long hair of young Victorian girls and was immortalised in Tenniel's illustrations for "Alice in Wonderland".

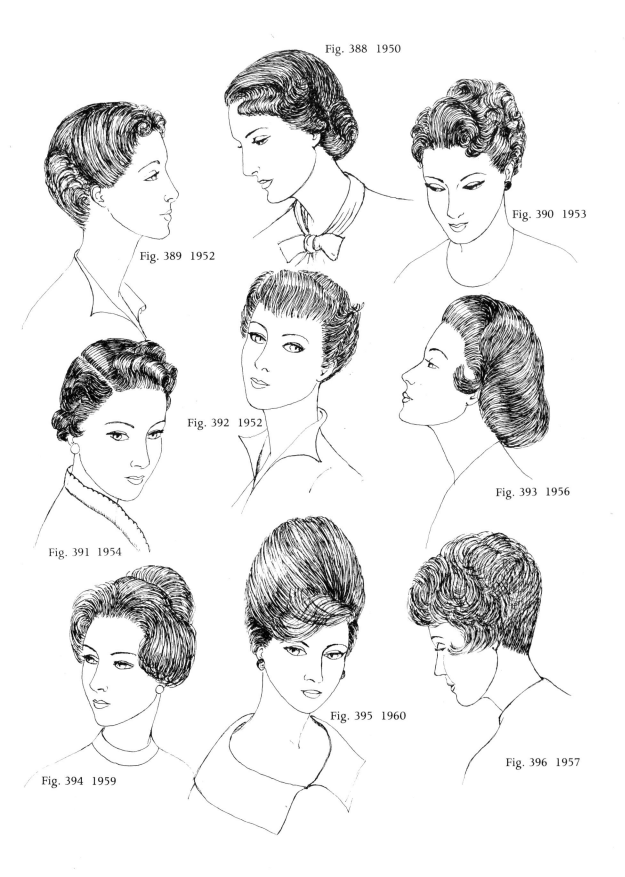

Fig. 388 1950

Fig. 389 1952

Fig. 390 1953

Fig. 392 1952

Fig. 391 1954

Fig. 393 1956

Fig. 394 1959

Fig. 395 1960

Fig. 396 1957

Twentieth Century

9 Hats 1950–1960

Off-the-face hats were still fashionable in the early 'fifties, but all styles and sizes were worn with a continuation of the side-to-side movement **(Fig. 397)**, or a side dipping movement. By 1952 small hats set straight on the head were coming into fashion **(Fig. 398)**, although little close-fitting cap styles hugging the back of the head were still very popular **(Fig. 399)**. For dressy occasions small "half hats" were much in vogue. These were oval or round shapes of straw or velvet curved and stiffened to fit snugly on top of the head **(Fig. 401)**. Sometimes the hat simply consisted of rings or loops of straw or stiffened fabric trimmed with flowers and veiling. For occasions such as weddings or cocktail parties a piece of veiling trimmed with a few little velvet bows or a large artificial flower might replace the more conventional hat. In general hats were very small and were of the pill box or *pancake* style set straight on the head **(Fig. 400)**, or the cloche and beret type set on the back of the head or slightly to the side. There were a few large hats of the sailor or coolie style **(Fig. 403)**.

The headscarf was still being worn by many women including members of the Royal family. With the return to formality in dress many affected to despise this "peasant" headwear as slovenly and unbecoming but, regardless of changing fashions in hairstyles it still retained its appeal as a comfortable and convenient covering for outdoor wear in cold, wet weather. Thousands of these scarves were produced in a wide variety of colours and patterns ranging from expensive designs in silk to cheap examples in nylon and other man made fabrics.

Fig. 397 1951

Fig. 398 1952

Fig. 299 1953

Fig. 400 1954

Fig. 401 1953

Fig. 402 1954

Fig. 403 1955

Twentieth Century

10 Hats 1950–1960

In the middle and late 'fifties small hats and rather flat large-brimmed hats continued to be in fashion, but styles with deeper crowns and set well forward on the brow were coming into vogue. "Flower pot" and squarish shapes with small brims or none at all were sometimes swathed in tulle or velvet **(Fig. 404)**. Towards the end of the decade fairly large dipped brims were the latest style to be introduced and for winter wear large fur hats **(Fig. 409)** were becoming extremely popular, as were all kinds of woolly caps. A variety of other hats was still being worn, including some with halo brims, and small close-fitting styles were still to be seen. The type of hat shown in **Fig. 406** was a favourite with many women, especially for summer when it was made like a large puff-ball of flowers, fancy straw, ruched net or chiffon. The example illustrated was made in pink beaver with a black satin band, but the most usual materials for hats during the post-war era were straw and felt with velvet, jersey, wool and fur for winter.

Although every woman who wished to wear a hat could be sure of finding a style to suit her, the post-war trend towards hatlessness was spreading rapidly. Women approaching middle age had become used to going without hats during the war and now found the novelty of the New Look and the post-war interest in hats wearing thin. Younger women, who had never acquired the habit of wearing a hat as an essential part of outdoor wear, tended to buy something soft and comfortable for winter or to acquire a hat only for special events such as weddings. Whatever the reasons for the decline in hat-wearing in everyday life most women seemed to feel that for special occasions at least a hat was still a necessity.

Fig. 404 1956

Fig. 406 1959

Fig. 405 1955

Fig. 407 1957

Fig. 408 1957

Fig. 409 1958

Fig. 410 1960

Twentieth Century

11 Hair and hats 1960–1972

The most remarkable trend in fashion during the 'sixties was the breaking down of formality and of many previously accepted standards. With increasing affluence at all levels of society, a constant demand for novelty and change was being created. Many extreme styles were seen during the decade. Skirt hems rose to heights never before seen or imagined. They swept the floor and rose again. Trousers in every kind of material and cut were seen on every occasion and at all times of the day. In general the maturer women tended to avoid the more exaggerated novelties, but the young adopted all the 'trendy' styles, many of which were designed exclusively for them and sold in shops which catered specially for the 'teenage' group.

The trend in dress was reflected in hairdressing, and every woman wore her hair in a style to suit her own taste and way of life. The most noticeable change in the hair of women of all ages was the softer and more casual styling. The older types of tight permanent wave had given place to methods which achieved a much more natural effect. The use of large rollers for setting gave the hair a slight lift which was particularly flattering to older women. The style shown in **Fig. 412**, with many slight variations such as soft waves or curls at the temples, became one of the most popular with women of all ages. The art of cutting was recognized as the most important of the hairdresser's skills, as also was the use of subtle tints for colouring the hair with a perfectly natural effect.

During the early 'sixties many girls in their teens allowed their hair to grow long, and although for school wear it was sometimes tied in a pony tail or two bunches on either side of the head, it was more often simply allowed to hang freely. In spite of adult disapproval and of condemnation by fashion pundits, who each year pronounced the fashion hopelessly outdated, the flowing hair remained popular, many girls and young women wearing it waist-length. Those of the younger generation who did not care for the inconvenience of long hair wore a variety of short styles, or compromised with longish hair in straight or curled bobs or tapered up and curled in layers. Women of all ages who had long hair might also choose to wear it in traditional manner in a bun or French pleat, or might draw it up in a coil or swirl of curls on the crown of the head (**Fig. 414**).

By far the most important news in hair over this period was the fashion for wigs and hair pieces, a trend which first started in the late 'fifties and developed into a worldwide business by the mid-'sixties. The best wigs were very expensive as they were made of the finest quality human hair, but those of man-made fibres were cheap and consequently were extremely popular. Wigs made of synthetic fibres could be easily washed, and being permanently shaped, they required no setting.

The decline in hat wearing already apparent in the 'fifties continued steadily. The hat industry was declared to be booming, but small milliners' shops dealing exclusively in headwear went gradually out of business and hats were now mainly sold in department stores. Hats still appeared on most heads at important social functions, but were rarely seen on the street. In the early 'sixties a favourite style of hat was the one shown in **Fig. 411**, and for summer wear a large toque made entirely of flowers, ruched net or chiffon was always fashionable. Fur hats enjoyed periodic popularity, and seemed particularly appropriate with the winter "midi" coats and boots of 1969–71. Berets, turbans, woolly hats and helmets in a variety of up-to-date shapes all appeared during the last years of the 'sixties, and a peaked cap known by various names was a favourite with younger women (**Fig. 416**). But by far the most distinctive types of hat seen during the later years of the period were the deep-crowned, wide-brimmed styles of decidedly masculine character, such as the Spanish, the trilby, the sombrero and the stetson (**Fig. 417**).

Fig. 412 1963

Fig. 413 1965

Fig. 411 1962

Fig. 414 1967

Fig. 416 1970

Fig. 415 1969

Fig. 418 1972

Fig. 417 1970–71

Fig. 419 1972

Twentieth Century

12 Hair 1972–1985

Much of what was said regarding hair styles in the previous chapter can be applied to the following years. Although clothing designers looked back for inspiration to the nineteen-twenties, 'thirties and 'forties, and hairdressers devised complementary styles, fashion remained very much a matter of personal taste. Most women continued to wear their hair and clothes in exactly the way they wished, to suit their increasingly liberated lifestyles, but as always the trends were there for those who wanted to follow them. A successful hairdresser needed to be a keen observer of feminine character without forgetting practicality and the client's taste.

The most important changes occurred in methods of cutting and in the considerable advances made in permanent waving technology. The use of a razor for cutting, once so prevalent, went out of favour, as did the practice of back-combing to give fullness to the hair.

A realization of the importance of the health and condition of the hair led to a flourishing market for hair-care products, including shampoos and conditioners for every hair type. The ingredients ranged from exotic oils or traditional herbal blends such as henna, camomile and rosemary, to others with very scientific-sounding names.

A need for additional texture and volume in styling led to the development of new setting agents. These gels and mousses helped to lift the hair and hold the set whilst maintaining the casual appearance characteristic of many of the newer styles.

The use of colourants was, of course, continued in the form of permanent dyes and bleaches. Temporary tints were easy to apply, incorporated in shampoos and setting agents or rinses. Although natural colours were preferred by the majority, other tints were to be seen, either over the whole head or on part of the hair only. Pink and occasionally daring combinations of bright colours were favoured by those who followed the fashion known as 'punk'. This was a so-called street fashion which appeared, apparently spontaneously, among the young in the late 'seventies (**Figs. 422** and **427**).

The short neat styles similar to that shown in **Fig. 419** continued well into the 'seventies, but with the fringe tending to be swept sideways and layered (**Fig. 420**). Long and short bobs, either with turned-under page-boy effect, or with upward flicks of curls, and many of the soft casual styles, were set by the blow-drying method instead of being put on rollers. This consisted of lifting and turning strands of hair over a brush whilst using a hand-held dryer.

The boyish or 'androgenous' cut was favoured by some younger women. This was introduced during the late 'seventies, becoming shorter and more extreme towards the mid-'eighties. It took various forms, being at first fairly long with soft curls or feathery strands over the top of the head and falling loosely forward, but gradually cropped heads were publicized, and adopted by more adventurous girls (**Figs. 428**, **430** and **431**). Another style popular with all age groups shows the backward and upward movement typical of many styles of this period, though there was a very noticeable trend for fringes or stray locks to fall over the forehead (**Fig. 426**).

Very long hair became something of a rarity, but for those who preferred it, some variations in ways of wearing plaits provided a change from the classical knots and coils.

The craze for wigs died away during the 'seventies, but they remained available in some department stores throughout the period. For pop stars, and other people in show business for whom an ever-changing image was important, a technique was devised in the 'eighties whereby very short cuts could be extended. Synthetic fibres were bonded to the natural hair in order to lengthen and thicken it. Glowing colours could be added without using dyes, and the results were claimed to last for several months.

It would be impossible to illustrate the enormous variety of styles made possible by the skill of the hairdressers at this time. With periodicals devoted entirely to the care and styling of hair and a vast range of products designed to improve and beautify, it would seem unlikely that women could ever again become slaves to any particular fashion.

Fig. 420
Mid 1970's

Fig. 421
1970's

Fig. 422
1976

Fig. 423
1970's

Fig. 424
1970's

Fig. 425
1980

Fig. 426
1980

Fig. 427
1982

Fig. 428   1981

Fig. 429
1984

Fig. 430
1984

Fig. 431   1984

Twentieth Century

13   Hats and Headwear 1972–1985

The decline in hat wearing of the 'fifties and 'sixties continued in the 'seventies and 'eighties in spite of the efforts of the trade and the fashion press. Every year designers produced a variety of styles, and many stores continued to maintain a hat department. Most women required hats for special occasions only, or perhaps for winter wear. It would seem that, in spite of the casualness of everyday clothing, the woman attending an important family or social event still felt that her outfit was not complete without a hat.

Stylish and sometimes extravagant hats continued to appear on traditional hat-wearing occasions such as the Ascot race meeting or Henley Regatta.

Members of the Royal family had always worn hats in public, and other women in leading positions usually did so when attending important functions. The Princess of Wales attracted a great deal of attention as a leader of fashion. From the time of her marriage in 1981 her clothes aroused exceptional interest in the fashion world. Her small hats were much copied by the trade. A chain of department stores claimed to have sold 18,000 of their version of the little tricorne she wore when going away on her honeymoon. **Fig. 436** shows an example of the type of hats favoured by the Princess in the early 'eighties. They were usually trimmed with feathers or flowers and sometimes with veiling. It is interesting to note that a small pill-box style worn by her in 1984 was precisely similar to one launched by the trade in 1979, an indication of how little fashions changed during this period.

From the early 'seventies onwards, traditional styles such as the turban, the beret and the trilby reappeared at intervals. The masculine shapes in evidence at the end of the previous period were again the most influential, and showed no sign of disappearing. Variations of the trilby were common, and as well as being made in felt, they were produced for the summer in pastel-coloured straw trimmed with ribbon and flowers. Straw boaters might be similarly decorated; also the Spanish hat with its flat shallow crown and wide brim. Small versions of the trilby in tweed or woven wool fabrics were to be seen during the winter. Knitted woolly caps similar to those worn in the 'sixties and early 'seventies were a popular form of headwear in cold weather, together with matching scarves. Wool berets in traditional form with a little stalk on the crown or attached to a leather head band were introduced in the mid 'seventies, and were also to be found in velvet or plaited ribbon or straw.

With few exceptions, most hats had fairly deep crowns which fitted comfortably on the head. They could have either small or broad brims turned down all round or perhaps turned up at the back, or the front, or were sometimes side-tilted in 1930's fashion. They appeared in various guises and materials. Made in plain or printed cotton, they were a useful addition to a holiday wardrobe **(Fig. 440)**. For smarter summer wear, those made of straw with large dipped brims made a regular appearance decorated with flowers, veiling or feathers **(Fig. 432)**.

A style known as a 'beanie' reminiscent of the 'twenties was designed in the early 'seventies. At first this took the form of a plain brimless cap pulled down to the eyebrows. Later, a small rolled or turned-up brim was added **(Fig. 439)**. These cloche-type hats were still being produced in the early 'eighties.

An attempt was made in the mid 'seventies to popularize the turban style in a variety of ways. Lengths of fabric were folded closely round the head and tied at the back or side. Triangular pieces had the ends tied behind the head or perhaps crossed over and brought forward to be knotted over the forehead. These and other more sophisticated versions were so arranged as to hide the hair completely. More turban styles, together with other types of headwear such as the coolie hat, were shown by the Paris designers in the spring of 1985.

A trend for wearing bandeaux, another 'twenties fashion, appeared in the late 'seventies. Although these might be a fairly narrow rigid band of a decorative nature, they were also made from rolled or twisted fabric and were probably found useful for keeping hair in place when taking part in the increasingly popular keep-fit and sporting activities.

Fig. 432
1975–1980's

Fig. 434   1982

Fig. 433
1978–1980's

Fig. 435   1976

Fig. 436
1983

Fig. 437   1980

Fig. 438   1970's–1985

Fig. 439   1978–1980's

Fig. 440
1975–1980's

Headwear of domestic servants and nurses

Although the custom of wearing indoor caps had almost entirely disappeared by 1880, this form of headwear was retained as a kind of uniform to be worn by domestic servants and waitresses for at least another 50 years, and by the nursing profession until the present day.

During the eighteenth and early nineteenth centuries maids generally wore versions of the fashionable caps of the period. For everyday work the mob was probably the most generally worn, continuing even into the twentieth century (**Fig. 443**). For afternoon wear or formal occasions in the late Victorian and Edwardian periods the maid would don a starched cap with long streamers similar to those worn by ladies in the 1860's and 1870's (**Fig. 441**). After the First World War maids and waitresses continued to wear some form of vestigial cap, one of the most usual styles being a band of pleated muslin threaded with ribbon (**Fig. 444**). This type was eventually superseded by wisps of fabric or by large bows perched on top of the head.

From the time of Florence Nightingale it was usual for nurses to wear some kind of white cap, the style of which, although varying from one hospital to another, also resembled those last worn by ladies about 1870. The streamers were usually tied under the chin in a bow. The brimless bonnets which accompanied the outdoor uniforms of capes or caped coats were also based on styles of the same period (**Fig. 447**). Nurses' headwear changed little until the First World War, although by that time the kerchief type of headcovering, and the style which was the forerunner of the modern nurse's cap, were becoming established (**Figs 445** and **446**). The grades of the nursing hierarchy have always been distinguished by variations in cap styles as well as by other distinctions in uniform, but these caps which would have become part of the insignia of the profession and the bows and frills which may still be seen on the heads of waitresses are the relics of a fashion of the mid-Victorian era.

Fig. 442 shows an example of a *boudoir* cap worn during the first quarter of the twentieth century. This was a kind of night cap or dressing cap used by some fashionable women.

Fig. 441 1894

Fig. 422 1913

Fig. 443 1904

Fig. 444 1932

Fig. 445 1917

Fig. 446 1917

Fig. 447 1895

Bridal headdress

The practice of crowning brides with chaplets of flowers originated in Anglo-Saxon times and may even be of earlier date, for in early Christian times both bride and groom were crowned in this way. Medieval brides were encouraged by the clergy to regard the garland with religious reverence and to prize the right to wear it as one of the privileges of their sex. It was of course, a symbol of purity and could only be worn by virgins. The chaplet could be made in various ways. In England, roses and sprigs of myrtle were for a long period its principal materials, and rosemary was also used. Garlands composed chiefly or entirely of ears of wheat, typical of fruitfulness, were worn in some districts at the end of the feudal period. Frequently the flowers and leaves were fitted on a circlet of metal and it was the custom in some parts of the country for the clergy and wardens of parish churches to provide coronets of metal for the ceremonial crowning of newly married women. The gilding of flowers and leaves for the adornment of brides and their attendants was also customary. Those of royal or noble birth usually wore crowns or jewelled coronets in place of the circlet of flowers.

For many centuries nothing was placed on the bride's head other than the chaplet and her hair was worn flowing loose as a sign of her maidenhood. Lady Jane Grey at her wedding to Lord Guilford Dudley wore her hair flowing over her shoulders and entwined with strings of pearls. Princess Elizabeth, daughter of James I, at her marriage to the Prince Palatine, was described as wearing her hair "hanging down her back, an ornament of virginity: a crown of pure gold upon her head the cognizance of majesty . . .".

The origin of the bridal veil is a disputed question which may never be settled. What has become the most conspicuous feature of the bride's attire may be nothing more than a substitute for flowing hair, the centuries-old symbol of virginity. It may have had its origin in the veil of the Hebrew marriage ceremony or the saffron veil or *flammeum* which was worn by the Greek and Roman brides. It may come from the same religious source as the veil which was used by Christians in the ninth century and which was at a later period made to envelop both the bride and groom during the wedding ceremony. Whatever its origins it was by no means universally worn at any period. After the end of the fifteenth century most girls would have been content to wear a new coif, cap or hat whilst the chaplet of fresh flowers remained the choice of the country girl. During the eighteenth century the wreath and veil went completely out of favour and were seldom worn by the fashionable. Instead, lace caps or hats were preferred. Horace Walpole's niece wore a hat for her wedding in 1759, and in 1788 a fashionable heiress wore a white satin hat with a white satin dress. Royal brides continued to wear jewels in their hair. On the occasion of her wedding to the Prince of Orange, the daughter of George II was described as wearing on one side of her head a pear-shaped green diamond of vast size and two pearls that were fastened to wires and hung loose upon her hair, and on the other side were small diamonds "prettily disposed".

However the "traditional" bridal wreath of orange blossom may have originated it is a custom of comparatively recent date in England. It was introduced from France about 1820, when the wealthy and fashionable began to wear special wedding attire with veil and wreath, and the idea was eventually copied at all levels of society. It is believed that the orange tree was introduced into Spain by the Moors, and one of several legends tells of the Spanish girl who was the first to wear a sprig of the blossom in her hair on her wedding day. The orange tree produces both fruit and flowers simultaneously and the white blossom may in earlier times have been considered an appropriate adornment for brides as it seemed to symbolize both purity and fertility. But even in Victorian times it was by no means a universal favourite and was often mixed with or replaced by other flowers or, for the wealthy bride, by a diamond tiara.

Since the First World War circlets or small caps, varying in style and material according to prevailing fashion and the social status of the bride, have rivalled the age-old flower wreath.

Fig. 448   *c.* 1744

Fig. 449   1806

Fig. 450   1858

Fig. 451   1870

Fig. 452   1918

Fig. 453   1936

Glossary

Aigrette, an upstanding ornament.

Apollo or Appollon knot, originated from the knot of hair on the head of a famous statue of the Greek god of that name.

Birdseye, a spotted muslin or silk.

Blond, lace made of silk.

Bobbin lace, made with bobbins by hand.

Bodkin (sixteenth century), a hair ornament in the shape of a long pin with a decorative top or jewelled pendant.

Bone lace, bobbin lace.

Cambric, a kind of fine white linen originally manufactured at Cambrai in Belgium.

Capercalzie, or capercaillie, the largest bird of the grouse kind.

Chignon, a large roll of natural or artificial hair worn at the back of the head.

Coque, a band of hair or a plait folded over to form a loop.

Crisped, curled.

Cutwork, openwork embroidery; the motifs were outlined in thread and then cut out. Used as a substitute for lace.

Cypress, a transparent lightweight lawn of gauze-like texture.

Frizzettes, small rolls of hair woven on to a wire frame and made up into sets of two or three.

Frizzled, frizzed, tightly curled hair.

Fustian, a material with a silky finish made from cotton or flax mixed with wool; much used as a substitute for silk.

Gauze, a very thin, transparent fabric made from silk, cotton or linen.

Goffered, crimped or fluted by means of a specially shaped iron.

Gros de Naples, a corded silk made in Italy.

Impeyan, Himalayan pheasant.

Kerseymere, a fine woollen cloth with a twilled finish.

Lettice, white or grey fur resembling ermine.

Miniver, variegated or banded fur, the choicest type available in the Middle Ages.

Muslin, a fine thin semi-transparent cotton of which there were many varieties.

Pynched, pleated.

Tiffany, a kind of gauze or thin silk.

Torsade, a hair piece consisting of a twisted two-stem swathe.

Toupée, a half wig constructed to cover the top of the head.

Vandyck or Vandyke, a lace collar or an edging shaped in points similar to those worn in the seventeenth century; called after Anthony Vandyke, the artist.

Venice gold, gold thread.

Sources of Information

Fashion Research Centre, Bath Museum of
  Costume
Bethnal Green Museum
Bodleian Library, Oxford
British Museum
Imperial War Museum
London Museum
National Gallery
National Portrait Gallery
Newspaper Library, Colindale
Platt Hall Gallery of English Costume,
  Manchester
Reading Public Library
Reading University Library
Tunbridge Wells Museum
Victoria and Albert Museum
Witt Library of Photographs, Courtauld Institute

Church sculpture, carving, monumental effigies
  and brasses
Paintings, miniatures and photographs
Fashion plates

Magazines and newspapers of the eighteenth,
nineteenth and twentieth centuries, including
the following:
Ackermann's Repository
The Gallery of Fashion
Hair and Beauty
Hairdresser and Beauty Trade
Hairdressing and Beauty
Hairdressing Fashions
Hairdresser's Journal
Harper's (Bazaar)
La Belle Assemblée
Le Journal des Costumes
Le Moniteur de la Mode
Le Petit Courier des Dames
Millinery
The Berkshire Chronicle
The Englishwoman's Domestic Magazine
The Hairdresser
The Ladies' Book of Fashion
The Ladies' Cabinet of Fashion

The Ladies' Gazette
The Ladies' International Fashion Magazine
The Lady's Magazine
The Ladies' Monthly Museum
The Ladies' Pocket Magazine
The Lady's Realm
The Ladies' Treasury
The Ladies' Wear Trade Journal
The Milliner and Dressmaker
The Millinery Record
The Reading Standard
Townsend's Fashions
The Queen
Vogue

Bibliography

A Handbook of Millinery, M. J. Howell, 1847

A Dictionary of English Costume 900–1900, P. Cunnington and C. Beard, 1960

A History of Costume in the West, F. Boucher, 1967

A History of English Costume, I. Brooke, 1949

A History of English Dress, G. Hill, 1893

A History of Everyday Things in England (4 vols) 1066–1914, M. and C. H. B. Quennell, 1956–63

A History of the Straw Hat Industry, J. G. Dony, 1942

Alabaster Tombs, A. Gardner, 1940

A Short History of Costume and Armour 1066–1800, F. Kelly and R. Schwabe, 1931

British Costume during Nineteen Centuries, C. H. Ashdown, 1929

Costume in Brasses, H. Druitt, 1906

Costume in England, F. W. Fairholt, 1909

Costume and Fashion, H. Norris, 1938

Costume du Moyen Age, J. van Bevoren and C. du Pressoir, Brussels 1847

Costume of the Western World, G. Reynolds, 1951

Cyclopaedia of Costume, J. R. Planché, 1874

Die Mode in der Menschlichen Gesellschaft, R. König and P. W. Schuppisser, 1958

Dresses and Decorations of the Middle Ages, H. Shaw, 1858

Dress and Habits of the People of England, J. Strutt, 1796

England as seen by Foreigners, ed. by W. B. Rye, 1865

English Costume, D. Yarwood, 1967

English Medieval Sculpture, A. Gardner, 1937

Englishwomen's Clothing in the 19th Century, C. W. and P. Cunnington and C. Beard, 1960

Elizabethan Pageantry, H. K. Morse, 1934

Fashion and Reality 1840–1914, A. Gernsheim, 1963

Fashions in Hair, R. Corson, 1965

Fashion in Paris 1797–1897, O. Uzanne, 1901

Handbook of English Costume (4 vols), C. W. and P. Cunnington, 1964–70

Hand-coloured Fashion Plates 1770–1899, V. Holland, 1955

Historical Costumes of England, N. Bradfield, 1970

History of Fashion, M. Fabre, 1966

Holbein Drawings at Windsor Castle, ed. by K. T. Parker, 1945

How did it begin?, R. Brasch, 1965

How to Dress as a Lady on £15 a Year, by A Lady, 1873

Le Costume Historique, A Racinet, 1888

Life and work of the People of England (6 vols), D. Hartley and M. Elliott, 1925–31

Monumental Brasses of England, C. Boutell, 1849

Monumental Brasses of Berkshire, H. T. Morley, 1924

Monumental Effigies of Gt. Britain, C. A. Stothard, 1823

Mundus Muliebris, M. Evelyn, 1690

Medieval Costume in England and France, M. G. Houston, 1939

Modes and Manners, M. von Boehn, 1935

Occupational Costume in England 11th century–1914, P. Cunnington and C. Lucas, 1967

Plocacosmos, J. Stewart, 1782

Progresses and Processions of Queen Elizabeth, ed. by J. Nichols, 1826

Sumptuary Legislation and Personal Regulation in England, F. E. Baldwin, 1926

Taste and Fashion, J. Laver, 1937

The Anatomie of Abuses in England, Philip Stubbes, 1583

The Art and Craft of Hairdressing, ed. by J. Bari-Woollss

The Changing Face of Beauty, M. Garland, 1957

The Costume of Great Britain, W. H. Pyne, 1804

The Diary of Fanny Burney

The Diary of Lady Anne Clifford

The Diary of Samuel Pepys

The Elizabethan Woman, C. Camden, 1952

The Fashionable Lady in the 19th Century, C. Gibbs-Smith, 1960

The History of the Hat, M. Harrison, 1960

The Ladies' Dictionary, 1694

The Ladies' Book, L. A. Godey, 1830

The Mode in Hats and Headdress, R. Turner Wilcox, 1959

The Paston Letters

The Romance of the Straw Hat, C. E. Freeman, 1933

The Strange Story of False Hair, John Woodforde, 1971

The Wheel of Fashion, M. Braun-Ronsdorf, 1964

The Victoria County Histories

Victorian Costume and Costume Accessories, A. M. Buck, 1961

Women's Dress 1730–1930, N. Bradfield, 1968

Index